The best garden: Revelation 22

Mom, Mr. Greathead, Julie, Margaret and Bev:
I thank you, and if the readers knew how much more readable you
made this book, they'd thank you, too!

I've got the best husband and kids in the world. Thanks, guys.

Simpleton Solutions

The Grocery Garden

How Busy People Can Grow Cheap Food

ELISE COOKE

Outskirts Press, Inc.
Denver, Colorado

The Grocery Garden
How Busy People Can Grow Cheap Food
All Rights Reserved.
Copyright © 2009 Elise Cooke
V3.0

Outskirts Press, Inc.
http://www.outskirtspress.com

ISBN: 978-1-4327-2395-8

Library of Congress Control Number: 2009921264

Outskirts Press and the "OP" logo are trademarks belonging to Outskirts Press, Inc.

PRINTED IN THE UNITED STATES OF AMERICA

Table of Contents

Introduction: Victory!

INTRODUCTION
Victory!

How empowering is it to grow your own food? Well, we won two world wars that way.

A Poster from WWI

With armies "marching on their stomachs," food quickly became scarce and even rationing wasn't sufficient to feed the soldiers and the home front. There were also shortages in labor, fuel, trucks and airplanes to transport food from farm to table. Enter the Victory Garden. Governments in the United Kingdom and United States issued a strident appeal to private citizens to plant fruits, vegetables and herbs anywhere they could.[1]

By 1944, nearly twenty million patriotic Americans had responded, producing upwards of forty percent of the produce consumed nationally, freeing up commercial crops to keep our forces fighting.

Fast forward to now. The hue and cry to renew the Victory Garden movement is coming from many voices; from Slow Food

---

[1] Of the many jobs my grandfather had during the Great Depression, one of them was scraping bird guano off of rocks for $.25 an hour, to be used as fertilizer.

advocates, to health experts, to the Green faction, to economists concerned about our high trade imbalance and to patriots concerned about all the foreign oil we burn to farm, fertilize and transport our food long distances.

The "call to arms" also issues from those concerned about alleviating food shortages throughout the world, debt-ridden householders cutting expenses, apocalyptic self-sufficiency types building up their larders for the Big One, and even from simple folks who just like the taste of fresh produce. Pick your worldview. A food garden fits into it quite comfortably.

While I may touch on some of the other issues, my enthusiasm for vegetable gardening boils down to this:

- Growing your own garden gives you a surprisingly-large amount of healthy food

- in a surprisingly-small space,

- involving surprisingly-little of your direct involvement,

- while saving you a surprising amount of money!

That's my personal struggle: the constant tug of effort versus outcome and nutrition versus expense. The purpose of this book is to prove the efficacy of a vegetable garden tactic in that fight. But, regardless of what trench you're in, growing your own food is a solid step on the path to winning your war.

Several studies estimate the average distance fresh vegetables travel from farm to table to be in excess of 1,500 miles.

Toward the end of his life, Thomas Jefferson wrote, "Though an old man, I am but a young gardener." A life-long and enthusiastic botanist, Jefferson lived into his eighties. Still, he felt that he had much more to learn when it came to cultivation.

I was reminded of Jefferson's humility while doing the research for this book. In too many cases, I would read from one source that a certain plant loved acidic soils, only to see it listed elsewhere as exactly the opposite. To solve any research discrepancies I encountered, I either drew from my own experience or went with the majority. I hate to start off a book with a big fat "caveat emptor," but the subject is so vast, no one has all the answers, at least not all the right answers. I have been growing food for most of the last twenty years, though. Most of my failures stem (pun intended) from the forehead-slappingly obvious, like neglected watering.

As that unswerving proponent of victory Winston Churchill once said,

> **"We shall [plant] on the beaches, we shall [plant] on the landing grounds, we shall [plant] in the fields and in the streets, we shall [plant] in the hills; we shall never surrender."[2]**

Onward to victory!

---

[2] Okay, the word might have been "fight," but we knew what he meant!

Part I
The Essentials

Before I started gardening with an eye toward really feeding my family, I read that it takes an acre of land to meet the food needs of forty people. If that's true, I wondered how many people I could feed with my teeny, tiny plots totaling about five hundred square feet. I did a little math. By my calculations, I'd be out in the hot sun turning dirt and pulling weeds just to get enough sustenance for half a person. Well, phooey. How discouraging.

And how untrue! Fortunately, I soldiered on, driven largely by my husband's love for tomatoes that taste better than the bag they came in, and the desire to demonstrate to the kids that food didn't just magically materialize under the fluorescent lights in grocery store display cases. To my giddy astonishment, I found that in short order the garden was the nearly-exclusive source of our vegetables. It also now contributes about a fifth of our fruit, with more coming as trees and vines mature. That doesn't leave land for grains and beans for drying, but those are relatively cheap and non-perishable. Fresh produce provides the biggest benefit, both nutritionally and economically, so I concentrate my efforts there.

Admittedly, the most labor you're going to have to expend is in the very beginning of the gardening experience. It's small wonder then that many people don't even bother to get their shiny-new shovels really dirty. In the next five chapters, we're going to concentrate on what's absolutely vital to growing food. These are: a positive attitude, sun, water, soil and a very few tools.

Chapter One is a recounting of all the reasons I can list why a vegetable garden is a good idea. Once you're revved up about the project, a thorough understanding of the basics saves a lot of time and heartache later.

Hang in there. You'll be glad you did!

Chapter One
The Pep Talk

Y ou're busy. The last thing you need is another hobby. Let's cut to the chase: What's in it for the person who'd rather spend more time eating vegetables than growing them?

How should you love gardening? Let me count the ways, in no particular order...

Nutrition: Organic fruits and vegetables that you pick out of the backyard and eat the same day are chock-full of vitamins, pesticide-free, often more exotic than what you can find in the grocery store, and they taste better. It's not unusual for the produce in the grocery store to be a week old. Vitamins degrade in the presence of light and heat, which they encounter during shipment and over time.

Exercise: We suburbanites tend to be heavier than those in other lifestyles. Big city folk walk more than we do. Country folk are outside more. Tending a garden is purposeful, productive whole-body aerobic exercise...a much better use of time than the human hamster routine on a treadmill.

Quality for the Kids: It's botany, horticulture, ecology, geology, entomology, vegetable-appreciation, patience, self-sufficiency, home economics, meal-planning, nutrition science, and just plain time together.[3]

Ecological: The human/animal relationship with plants is purely symbiotic. Just about everything we expel, plants can use. We consume what's edible and breathe the oxygen they give us in return. This handshake agreement has worked between us for a long, long time.

Much of the commercial agricultural industry has become dependent on petroleum-based fertilizers and gasoline-powered machinery to farm the land. The carbon footprint of the corporate farm is larger than one would believe. You will need neither of those in order to work your garden.

Large farms also have to use tons of chemical weapons because they often plant the same crop year after year, in large quantities that attract and breed large numbers of hungry pests. These pesticides seep into the local water supply, poison beneficial insects along with the unwanted ones, and ultimately make their way into our food supply, too.[4] Your children, by contrast, will be able to eat your produce straight from the plant, and you won't have to worry about it.

There's been much concern lately about monocultures driving out variety in seed stocks. For generations, commercial growers have been developing crop strains that meet the needs of large-scale production, like produce firm enough to withstand the rigors of transport, higher specific pest resistance, greater yield. Did you hear "higher nutrition" anywhere in that list? That priority takes a back seat to the majority. In the competitive marketplace, however, this means that ultimately fewer and fewer varieties of crops are being grown. We're losing a lot of genetic diversity in our staples, making us more vulnerable to some superbug that can wipe out a whole segment of our food supply. If you're a home gardener, you're helping to maintain variegated subspecies of food crops.

Gardening and composting go hand-in-hand. By composting, you're diverting yard waste and garbage that would otherwise go into a

---

[3] Oh, heck; sometimes it's even discipline. If your kids do something wrong, point out a plot they can weed, while they reflect on the importance of making better choices next time.

[4] To be fair, farms are carefully regulated to minimize the excess runoff from dangerous pesticides. City runoff is much more polluting because some home gardeners apply high concentrations of chemicals to their crops. Please try a completely organic approach. You won't be disappointed!

landfill or have to be transported somewhere offsite and processed.

I harped on this before: Commercially grown food has to be transported, usually long distances while being stored in refrigerated trucks and warehouses. One of the easiest ways to lower your own carbon footprint is to eat as locally as possible. If your food source is so local that shoes are optional to go out and get it, even better!

Convenience: This one may not have occurred to you, but once a garden is established, it's so easy to use! Why run to the store, when your fresh produce is just outside? Through most of the year, my routine in the morning is to set a small hunk of meat on the counter to thaw, then take a colander outside to pick whatever we need for the day. Admittedly, this is somewhat offset by having to maintain the garden in the first place, but sticking something in the ground beats finding a parking space, listening to muzak, and struggling with the wayward wheel on that shopping cart, right?

Gifts: Everyone eats! Okay, this is not exactly news, but the garden yields wonderful gifts throughout the year. In the spring, hand out "truck gardens" of potted plants that you started inexpensively from seed, that will be, nonetheless, much appreciated. In the summer, your surplus produce will make everyone smile. In the autumn, give apples, pumpkins and squash, or make pies from them first. Even in the winter, you can put ribbons around your canned goods, dried fruits and flavored vinegars and oils for Christmas.

National Security: There's something in gardening for the patriotic, even if the government isn't asking us to take up the cause for the war effort. First and foremost, we're doing our little bit to lessen our dependence on foreign energy sources, some of which are funneling the money they get from us to fund activities that run counter to our interests.

One thing we have that the rest of the world envies and needs is our abundant ability to grow food. Witness our (and Europe's) sudden interest in diverting much of our corn crop into ethanol and what havoc that is wreaking on other economies, notably Mexico. Crop failures and unrest in other areas have heightened food insecurity in many places around the world. When the people can't eat, governments fall, usually to be replaced by radicalism. We ignore the hungry in the rest of the world, to our peril. Remember Marie Antoinette's famous response to the peasants' lack of bread?[5] In any case, more food aid from the United States would ameliorate food shortages elsewhere, which would in turn ease tensions.

Here's a fun fact to keep you up at night. The United States became a net food importer in 2005. We had a $13.6 billion surplus in 2001. Whether you place the blame on suburban sprawl, ethanol production, or anything else, regaining our self-sufficiency in food is vital to our national security. You can contribute in a positive way to this effort by cutting your consumption of commercial produce.

Macroeconomics: The U.S. trade imbalance with other countries is atrocious any way you want to look at it. Food beyond our domestic needs is one thing we can produce for export to help even out the deficit.

U.S. Trade Deficit:
2006: $763.6 Billion
2007: $711.61 Billion
2008: $677B

Commercial farms get squeezed on two fronts when the price of oil goes up. Their fertilizers are largely made from petrochemicals, and tractors don't run behind draft horses anymore! The good news is that you don't need either one to work your plot. The bad news, I guess, is that you can't apply for farm subsidies from the Department of Agriculture.

Microeconomics: As far as your personal pocketbook is concerned, your home-grown food can benefit you financially in many ways.

First, your efforts will give you a decent, nontaxable "wage" through savings on food. Exactly how much is hard to quantify, but we can take a stab at it. Let's say that each member of your family eats a pound of fruits and vegetables each day.[6] Furthermore, assume you could grow a garden to supply just half of your daily consumption. Now let's say that the average cost of each pound of the food is two dollars at the grocery store, and one-tenth that to grow it,[7] rendering a total

---

[5] "Let them eat cake!" Apologists for her insist that she was suggesting that the fancier bread be sold at the same price as the regular. Still others insist she didn't say it at all. But the peasants sure got fired up about it, regardless of the truth. Which brings us to our next lesson about starving people; they are lousy fact-checkers.

[6] This is slightly more than the recommended 400 grams, or 14 ounces in five servings that is the current wisdom.

[7] I didn't pull that one-tenth figure out of my head. A few seed vendors on-line came up with it first, and my own rudimentary calculations for my garden aren't

savings of $3.60 a day for a family of four. Yearly savings in this case: $1,314.

Second, even if you don't open your own booth at a farmer's market with your surplus, you have something to contribute amongst your network of friends. Again, the monetary reward here is hard to quantify, but it's real. Beneficiaries of my garden surplus have responded in kind with everything from used clothing and household goods to baled straw. In just clothing, including shoes and jackets, I save easily $250 per kid per year. The average two-child family with similar benefits would save another $500.

Third, don't ignore the savings from gifts. This was a point earlier, but it bears mentioning again. What if each of your kids' teachers and coaches got some nice pies from you, totaling maybe $2 each in expenses, instead of $10 gift cards? Would that save you $100 right there?

Fourth, there is a savings that simply comes from not finding yourself in the wrong place at an impulsive time. You didn't go to the mall for entertainment, your family was planting potatoes that Saturday morning. You didn't have to run to the grocery store that week, so you missed the "sale" on blueberry-flavored toaster pastries. I'm not even going to try to put a number on that one, but it's worth a mention.

Fifth, gardens have a tendency to keep you home and out of restaurants because the meals practically plan themselves based on what's available. Plus, no one can complain that there's "nothing to eat." Even if you miss only one fast-food trek a month, for a family of four, that'll work out to $400 a year.

Sixth, imagine the savings from the delayed onset of cancer, diabetes, heart trouble and any of a myriad other "lifestyle" health issues, due to your habit of healthy eating and moderate exercise while gardening: Priceless.

Self-Sufficiency: Even if you're not certain the end is near, it's nice to have a supply of food in case something bad closes the stores for a few days. We have to think about these things over here in Earthquake Country. (Granted, if your garden is flooded, burned, irradiated or whipped away in a tornado, this is a moot point.)

---

too far off of that. For instance, a single plant with 30 tomatoes worth $1 apiece works out to $30 worth of food for the cost of seed and water, i.e. about $.20, far less than that one-tenth figure. Carrots won't be quite so economical, a dollar's worth of seed grows about $10 worth.

Conversation: Go ahead and laugh, but I guarantee you'll be more interesting at dinner parties. It sure beats talking about politics!

Stress Reduction: I have a story that is a long-winded roundabout way of making my point, but bear with me.

Once upon a time, during my college years, I worked for a big retail chain. Not many clerks could speak Spanish, so even my weak, non-native skills were much in demand. In that vein, I was helping a customer one day, and had nearly completed the transaction, when he stopped me cold with, "I'll take my purchase, but I don't need the *gancho*."

Blinking in confusion, I queried "Um, is there a problem?"

"Oh no, I just don't want the *gancho*."

"So, uh, the size is fine?"

Amusement twinkled in his eyes. He was starting to have fun with me. "Everything is fine, except for the *gancho*. You can take the *gancho* back."

Well, this went on and on. In my best school Spanish, I inquired if the *gancho* had anything to do with the color, style, length, depth or anything else that came to mind. Now he was grinning from ear to ear.

Finally, once I'd exhausted myself, he asked. "So, do you want to know what a *gancho* is?"

"Yes please," I panted.

He silently picked up the hanger on which his clothing had recently hung. I smacked my forehead, hard. We both laughed until our sides split.

A few weeks later, corporate management announced that they wanted contributions to the company newsletter especially of a "light-hearted" nature. I thought this story fit the bill perfectly, so I typed up my submission and turned it in.

I was summoned to The Office a few days later. The Director for the entire District, which encompassed the whole northern part of California, greeted me with that simpering "professional courtesy" look. "Elise. How nice to see you. Please. Have a seat."

She coolly appraised me for a moment. I sat, bewildered, wondering what I'd done to attract this kind of attention to myself. With another flick of the Corporate Facial Spasm, she began. "We just wanted to get a chance to meet you, to get a sense of your values . . . and whether they match up with the values of the Big Box Family."

Oh no. I'd offended the whole Family. Did I forget to punch my timecard? Did I incorrectly count the change from the registers? Really, is it a crime to converse with the mannequins after hours?

She held up my newsletter submission with the tips of her long fingernails, as if she'd catch something from it. "Exactly what did you intend to say with this piece?"

Somehow, my boy-is-my-Spanish-awful-and-someone-got-the-better-of-me-for-it little ditty managed to trip one of the Big Box corporate law department's ethnic discrimination alarms. Madame District Director was clearly leaning toward protecting the Company

> I only took one sociology class in college, but it was all about the Culture of the Corporation. It was interesting to learn that just by calling itself your "Family," companies could inspire loyalty and longer hours without having to increase pay.

from a multi-billion dollar class action lawsuit by firing me on the spot and holding a press conference to trumpet the corporation's devotion to Tolerance and Diversity. And light-heartedness.

Okay, so my day in the hot seat wasn't exactly Martin Luther before the Diet of Worms. But it was stressful. Would that I'd had a little plot to call my own back then, because gardening is a huge stress-reliever!

This is your garden. You get to plant what you want, where you want, how you want. You see progress and actual results. You reap the rewards. It's so pleasant and so peaceful; your own world away from the world. If your life is crazy, consider a garden before therapy or an expensive vacation. Go outside, survey your blessings, and feel your blood pressure drop.

I'm sure I missed mentioning some aspect of vegetable gardening, but I'm equally sure it'd be on the "plus" side of the column. Of all the decisions to make, growing food, no matter how little, is an easy one.

Ready to get dirty?

Chapter Two
Weather For Art Thou

Plants get nutrients from the soil, but not their energy. The real food for the plant comes from electromagnetic radiation emanating from the sun, using an amazing metabolic pathway called photosynthesis, which converts light energy into chemical energy, specifically triose phosphates. These in turn can be rearranged into sugars, more complex carbohydrates or cellulose, whatever the plant needs.

> The condensed version of the photosynthetic reaction is:
>
> $$6\ CO_2 + 6\ H_2O + photons \rightarrow C_6H_{12}O_6 + 6\ O_2$$
>
> In English: carbon dioxide, water and light energy convert to glucose and oxygen.

Every living organism ultimately relies on this energy for survival by ingesting plants or plant-eaters, with the exception of some sulfur-sucking, bottom-dwelling scum in the ocean. I figure this latter fact might be useful for my readers who are still in high school.

He: "Hey, Babe, you're not mad about that two-timing thing, are ya?:

She, shaking her head slowly in mock sympathy: "You can't help it. A guy like you could starve if you get too far away from your hydrothermal vent."

He: "Yeah, that's...huh?" She walks away with her head held high while the Science Nerds at the next lunch table shoot milk out of their noses and roll on the floor.

Ah, well, maybe not. Moving on, the upshot of all this is that your vegetable crops need sun, lots of it. Less sunlight means less food to the plant, which means less food for you. Most plants do best with a minimum of six hours a day of direct exposure.[8] DO NOT attempt to dig a plot without first making sure the area can support vegetables with adequate sunlight. Too much shade cannot be corrected with more fertilizer, water, scarecrows, music, rain dances, crystal energy or anything else. It's called a "farmer's tan" for a reason. Also, factor in how tall plants will grow and if they'd effectively shield other plants from adequate sunlight, then plant the short ones where they won't be shaded.

If you've looked around and it's not possible to grow vegetables anywhere on your property, you have a few other possibilities:

- Neighbors' yards

- Vacant lots, although you should try to contact the owner for permission

- Community garden plots, which also often provide free water, advice and seed

- Simulate the sun's electromagnetic energy with special lights, called grow lights. These used to be hideously expensive, but now with LED technology, they're getting much cheaper to purchase and operate, and might one day soon be economically viable.

- Have you considered ripping out those hedges? They're pretty and all, but you can't eat them.[9]

---

[8] I've read that asparagus can get by on just four, but that doesn't fit my personal experience.

[9] For example, one on-line offers a slightly-larger-than square foot light for about $40, with an expected lifetime of 50,000 hours, then purports that it only requires 13.8 watts to run, which means it would run for a full 3 days before it even burned

- Have you also considered gardening in containers? You really can grow an amazing amount of food, with no weeds and very little water this way.

The other vital part of the growing equation is to know your local climate. "Climate" encompasses everything from lowest and highest temperatures, day length by date, average rainfall, humidity, and so forth. Specific crops need to grow in a particular temperature range. Plant too early, and some seeds won't even sprout in the cold weather, but they will get waterlogged and ruined while they're waiting. Plant a cool-weather crop in the late spring, and it's likely to bolt[10] and go bitter in the hot summer sun before it's of any use to you. Plant a warm-weather crop in the early autumn, and watch it sprout all right, then wither and die with the first cold snap.

Some plants are just a bad idea for your climate altogether. I never like to be the bearer of bad news, but if you live in North Dakota, backyard pineapple is not an option.[11] I understand cabbage grows to the circumference of hula hoops in Alaska, but when I tried to cultivate them in my moderate temperatures, the heads took about nine months to grow to the size of my fist. I can only imagine cabbage in Florida gets mistaken for Brussels sprouts.

The amount of sun in various parts of the intended space is easy enough to figure out; just stand outside at various times of the day and note where the shade travels. Note that the sun will be lower in the sky on a winter day than on a summer day, so try to get a sense of where the light will fall during the actual growing season. Determining climate is a little tougher, since it's based on average high and low temperatures throughout the year.

I have information that will, momentarily at least, make you feel good about paying taxes. The federal government has compiled

---

up a single kilowatt. At $.30 per kilowatt hour, it would cost about $3.57 per month in electricity and purchase price. Can you grow food for more than that, with the light? Depending on the crop, yes.

[10] To "bolt" is to send up a shoot with a flower stalk. Because so much energy goes into that effort, the rest of the plant usually turns bitter and tough, especially lettuce and spinach.

[11] This is unless you want to devote enormous amounts of time and money to tend the trees in a heated, humidified greenhouse, of course.

a wonderful interactive map that provides information about the climate in every part of the entire United States, Canada and Mexico. Climate zones are defined by their average annual minimum temperature, and then numbered. You need to learn your USDA Plant Hardiness Zone, because these are the gold standard by which most seed companies reference their recommendations for particular vegetables.

The USDA Plant Hardiness Zone Map is available at: http://www.usna.usda.gov/Hardzone/ushzmap.html

But wait, private enterprise does one better. Sunset Magazine's Garden Climate Zones detail not only the lowest low temperatures you can expect in your area, but inform as to what kinds of plants do best outside the whole year through. Be sure to make a note of that zone as well, since gardening forums on-line often remark on both the USDA zones and Sunset's.

To see the Sunset's Garden Climate Zones, go to: http://www.sunset.com/sunset/garden/article/0.20633.845218.00.html

Both of the above resources are good for general information and knowing where the "bottom" is in temperatures for your area, but it's also useful to be able to plan, as much as anyone can, what to plant and when. For instance, if I want tomatoes, and know that they prefer weather well past the danger of frost, and nighttime temperatures above 50F/10C degrees, when can I start them indoors a few weeks early and then transplant them outside? That question is a bit murkier to answer, but here are some resources:

Seed Packets. Read these for at least some cursory instructions on when to plant the crop outside. Usually these will guess at how warm your temperatures will be with phrases like "plant six weeks after last frost date." This isn't very accurate, but if you're in the zone specified on the packet and that's all the time you have, you'll probably come out all right.

Your neighbors. Chat up the old-timers with the big blooming yards. They're never wrong.

Annual Averages. The National Weather Service keeps statistics on monthly average temperatures as well as last year's data on its website. That's at nws.noaa.gov. Look in the Monthly Temps in the Climate section. There's also useful information at Intellicast.com. Enter your zip code and you can drill down from there to see the Historic Averages for your area. Of course, there's no guarantee that this won't be the Year of the Freak August Frost, but at least you're gambling with the house odds, so to speak.

Forecasts. Weather websites will often make predictions for upwards of a few months out. Be aware that these are just educated guesses.

Farmer's Almanac. I admit I've never bought one, but some people swear by it. Their website touts an eighty percent accuracy rate. Run an Internet search to find out more.

There'll be more on planning later, but the purpose in this chapter is to emphasize the importance of weather in having a vegetable garden that will produce enough food cheaply for your family to be worth the effort you'll have to put into it. The only way to minimize effort and expense in this and any endeavor is to first figure out the best way to do it. A little knowledge about your sunlight and temperatures will help you choose plants well suited for your circumstances. Failure to cooperate with your weather patterns in choosing what and when to plant will just set you up for more work, more capital outlay, more pests and other blight, and less productivity right from the start. So take a little time to do the research now, and you'll save yourself a headache down the line.

Chapter Three
Water You Doing?

'm a California girl, and proud of it. Blessed as we are with our mostly Mediterranean-like climate and fertile soils, we are the nation's largest agricultural state, to the tune of over $31B in products each year. We grow more than half of the nation's fruits, vegetables and nuts from less than four percent of the nation's farmland.[12]

But what California doesn't have in abundance is water. Now take out your pencils, it's time for a quiz. Recall the simplified photosynthetic reaction from the last chapter. How many molecules of water are required to produce each molecule of glucose? Anyone? Anyone?

The answer is six. So, is water important to growing food? (If you said "no," you flunked.)

You can see just how important water is to California agriculture by driving down Interstate 5 in the Central Valley region. Wending alongside as you travel past the many fruit and nut trees, grape vines, sheep, cows and field crops is a thin, concrete-lined ribbon of water. That's the California Aqueduct. Think of it as a giant straw, sucking fluid from the delta region in the northern part of the state outside of

---

[12] California, the Land of Fruits and Nuts! This state also produces 31% of the nation's dairy.

Sacramento and drawing it all the way down to the Los Angeles basin, 444 miles south of there. Along the way, farms take what they need to make the deserts bloom.

To say that Californians are obsessed with water isn't quite right. "Obsessed" is just too mild a word. Here's how the pre-wedding scene in *Monte Python and the Holy Grail* between Herbert and his father would have played out if we'd made that movie:

Herbert: "But I don't like her!"

Father: "You don't like her? What's wrong with her? She's beautiful, she's rich, she's got ripe...arian rights..."[13]

Ours is a constant tug of war to divide our water between the farms, the fish in the Delta Region and the burgeoning population of over 30 million people, and we're always short somewhere. That's why you'll sometimes see signs in public restrooms asking you not to flush unless you have a, um, solid reason.

I bring up all this about my home state for a couple of reasons. First, mine is not the only area where water is a precious commodity. Vast swaths of the Mid- and Southwest experience periodic severe drought as well, and in the rest of the world, literally billions of people are affected by water scarcity. I am fairly certain that wherever you are, conservation should play some part in your vegetable garden thinking.

Water is, not surprisingly, getting increasingly expensive. Home gardeners may start to wonder if they're really saving money on their grocery bill if their water bill gets much higher.

At the same time, water is not at all something your plants can skimp on without you losing a great deal of potential food. I can't stress this enough. All the fertilizer and sunlight in the world cannot make up for the lack of water. Here are some ways to water effectively and efficiently.

Water at the roots. There is no gain by spraying the leaves,[14] which will either encourage molds and other blight, or evaporate away. Letting water run down the pathways and everywhere else

---

[13] At the risk of making the joke not funny anymore, but understood, the term "riparian rights" refers to the system by which water source is legally allocated among nearby landowners.

[14] Some gardeners do swear by foliar sprays, which are dilutions of fertilizers sprayed directly on the plants to be taken up by the leaves. I can't usually be bothered to do this, but I will mention a couple of them throughout this book if you'd like to give them a try.

only benefits the weeds.

Water deeply, but less often. The idea here is that you want to encourage your plants to grow deep roots, where they will find more water for a longer period of time. To accomplish this, water until the moisture reaches a foot or so in depth. Check the soil again after three or four days. So long as the soil is moist several inches down, you're fine. Once the soil is almost dry at the same depth, you should water again.

Water consistently. Plants don't do well drowning one day and wilting the next. But far be it for me to suggest that you need to check constantly for water needs. Once you establish about how soon the soil will lose its moisture, establish a schedule and stick to it.

Mulch. Mulch is simply a cover of some sort over the dirt in your garden, the purpose of which is to block the dirt from the sun as much as possible. Mulch slows water evaporation from the soil. There are a number of different kinds of mulches, which is why it gets longer treatment later. But for now, consider it as a vehicle for water savings.

Consider installing a "drip system." Also known as "watering systems," these are basically multiple small hose lines that very precisely dedicate a prescribed amount of water exactly where you want it, and nowhere else. There are pros and cons to using them, but if cost and time are considerations, the balance is mostly positive. They deserve more explanation than the space here; see below for more detail.

Use your water twice. Shampoos and soaps are not usually harmful to plants; in fact, most shampoos contain phosphates, which are good fertilizers. This means that the water from your shower (and washing machine) is ideal for use in your garden, if you can figure out a convenient way to get it there. Do not reuse water from your toilet; though your plants would be happy, the bacteria are a health hazard to you.

Get water for free. Run a search on the Internet and read about all kinds of clever water catch-and-storage systems for rain. I was particularly intrigued by the story of a plumber who kept a line of old water heaters along one side of his house. He then rerouted his gutters to fill them up when it rained. In the dry season, he could draw from them. He even painted the water heaters to match the house so the system wasn't too obtrusive.

Stop leaks right away. That toilet that keeps running, the faucet that drips, and the leaky hose are all wasting an amazing amount of water, which translates to money down the drain. (Those of you with free, abundant well water can stop snickering now.)

Save household usage for the garden. Develop good, efficient water savings habits at home so you can devote more water for growing food. All the usual reminders are in play: Don't leave the water on when you brush your teeth. Save the water that you use when you're waiting for it to get hot. Take shorter showers. And so forth. And so on. You know all this. Now do it.

Even if you pay high rates for your water usage, you can save money growing your own food if you're careful. Certainly, some vegetables are more cost effective with the water issue versus others. Tomatoes, for instance, require only moderate amounts of water once they are established, and they cost so much at the store that it is very worthwhile to grow them. Carrots are less so, but even calculating for my high rates, I come out ahead. Water will be one of the more expensive inputs to your garden, so adopt as many conservation habits as early on in the process as possible.

As mentioned earlier in the chapter, the ultimate in water conservation for the garden has got to be a drip system. They are fast becoming the popular thing around here, even for shrubs. The advantages to these are legion:

There's that water thing again. You save a lot of water by bringing it directly to the specific places you want it, and nowhere else. If you take out plants and don't replant right away, then you can turn off the water to that particular area without affecting the other areas.

You can quantify exactly how much water you're using. Say your emitter allows 8 gallons of water per hour, and you water four beet plants per emitter for 20 minutes every three days until they mature at 45 days. If you pay $.004 per gallon of water, how much does each beet cost you to grow?[15] Now share your belabored calculations at the next dinner party you attend. Or not.

It promotes even watering, and metered watering for specific needs. Suppose you plant sunflowers, which need practically no water, next to peppers, which drink like fish. Put a very restrictive

---

[15] Four cents. Now say the beets leave on a train to Chicago, going west at 55 miles per hour…

emitter at the base of the drought-tolerant plant, and a large-capacity one at the base of the peppers. Now when you water, the right amount of water goes to each plant at the same time.

It saves time, too. Yes, really. If you set it up just where you need it every time you plant, then to water your garden, all you have to do is to turn it on. Walk away; do something else, and when you've watered enough, turn it off again. This sure beats standing around with a hose. Also, with some vine-like plants, it's hard to remember exactly where the roots are, so you end up having to water the whole area. With a static hose placed at the base, this is a non-issue.

It's reusable. These things are pretty sturdy. So far most of mine is still working after three years of use. When you're done with one crop, you can just move the hoses and emitters to another.

These things do have their disadvantages, too:

They cost money. I just did a quickie search and found a kit purporting to provide enough coverage for 220 square feet. It costs about $50, including tax and delivery. So the question is, how much water would I have to save in order to make this worth my while? Well, I pay $.004 per gallon, so the answer is 12,500 gallons. Hmmm. That seems like a lot and therefore if the economic argument is the only one of interest to me, this may not be worth it.

However, more math helps here. The claim is that with a "properly installed" drip system, you'll save upwards of 55% of your water. Okay, then. I'll assume I could grow 220 plants, one for each square foot, and keep the plot in constant cultivation for nine months out of the year.[16] I'll further assume that I'd water through 8 gallons-per-hour emitters for 20 minutes, every three days, over those 270 days, for a total of 90 gallons per square foot. 90 gallons times 220 square feet equals 19,800 gallons. If, as the "experts" claim, I'd waste that much over again without a drip system, then the $50 investment will save me almost $80 in water in just the first year. Furthermore, in my experience, I only need to replace about $5 in original equipment each year, so I come out way ahead.

Buyer beware! If you shop on-line or in a hardware store, it's easy to get taken in by all the gadgets and doodads available for these systems, and before you know it, you've blown your whole food budget. Keep the basics in mind. You want something to attach

---

[16] I'm in Zone 9, so that's not off-base.

to your faucet or hose that will split the water into several smaller sources. You want tubing. And you want whatever will get the water out of that tubing the best way for the plants you will grow.[17] Not everyone needs pressure regulators, backflow preventers, sensors and other spiffy stuff. Start small. You can always grow from there.

They take time to set up. Whole books are written on how to plot, plan, diagram and research your watering system. I avoided doing it for a couple of years, put off by the perceived complexity alone. Then, in a moment of clarity, I grabbed one end of a three-quarter inch hose, screwed on a hub with eight separate one-quarter-inch outlets, pushed one-quarter inch tubing onto each one, and I was good to go.

I then moved the tubes to the plants, and wherever I encountered one, I cut the tube, reattached the ends on either side of an emitter and there was my water source for that plant. Rocket science this is not, but to read some books or to look at all the equipment choices, you'd think it is. Still, initially making all those cuts and attaching all those emitters is a pain. The good news is that when you set it up next year, you can just put your plants where the emitters are, not the other way around.

They can, and probably will, leak. With my high water pressure, I sometimes get one of the tubes popping off of the hub. Also, at the juncture of the hub and hose or faucet, I'll sometimes get leakage. Buy a fresh roll of plumber's tape each year.

They break. Most parts are pretty sturdy, but they're in the elements practically all year long, so anything made of hard plastic eventually cracks, especially the ends of emitters. Also, the screw valves that turn the water off and on for individual tubes on the top of the hub are often made of this cheap, soft plastic that get wrecked if you turn them too much. Grrrr.

Drip systems actually can be a way to save time and money when growing your own food, but they take an investment in time and money to accomplish that. Still, if you want to grow a vegetable garden as cheaply and effortlessly as possible, consider at least a

---

[17] Drip systems also sell short pieces of plastic tubing for the express purpose of holding a crimped watering tube. Buy a few of these. Rubber bands for holding the crimped tube rot in short order, and then you're hosing water out of the end instead of through your emitters, d'oh! However, these pieces of tube that hold the crimp work just as well at half their length, so cut them to size and save some money.

simple drip system.

Soaker hoses, those hoses that leak all over on purpose, are not as precise and cost almost as much as a drip system. However, if they're laid at the roots of a row of plants, they'll direct water where it's needed.

In the "olden days," I'd do what some farms still do: run water down furrows alongside the plants. While that ultimately does get some of the water to the roots, the furrows need constant maintenance to repair breaches of the lines. They also take up valuable garden space. Water is also lost through gravity through the soil.

Plumber's tape is a thin, non-sticky waterproof tape that comes in a roll sort of like bandage tape. Roll a couple of thicknesses of this stuff on the threads of wherever there is leakage, then screw it back together, and that usually seals the leak, at least for a while.

As in the previous chapter, the main objective here is to think through how the critical inputs to the garden will be adequately supplied. Last chapter, the concern was enough sun; in this chapter it's water. The next chapter covers the last vital input: soil. These are the three legs that hold up a garden. Understanding the basics of each will save you much frustration later.

Chapter Four
Down and Dirty

O nce you've placed your plot somewhere where the sun can see it, you don't ever have to concern yourself with sun issues again. Get a good rhythm going for watering, and that's covered. The medium that plants grow in, however, is constantly being depleted of some aspect of its fertility as the vegetable plants take in nutrients from it for their own needs. Types of plants require differing amounts of minerals. Varieties of the same crop even vary in their nutrient needs. This is why fussy garden books wax obsessive on every kind of soil supplement imaginable.

I often wonder if some of these books are in league with fertilizer companies because they seem to recommend the most expensive and obscure materials imaginable and hype them as the only reasonable way to grow anything. In earlier days, when I was a bigger sucker, I got up from my reading and rushed to a specialty garden boutique. Breathlessly, I asked for green sand[18] as if life itself hung in the balance. Lucky for me, they'd never heard of the stuff, or I would have forked over my funds to the Prissy Plant Pavilion, none the wiser that maybe, just maybe this wasn't the vital substance the book

---

[18] Green sand is a natural, organic mined mineral that provides a bit of potassium, and helps break up clay soils. In other words, you can pay over a buck a pound to do what fallen leaves will do for free.

purported it to be.

So, what *is* important and what isn't? You'd think after thousands of years of cultivation, the science on that question would be settled, but we don't have all the dirt on dirt, yet, at least not on every single aspect of what optimal combination of minerals works best for each individual crop. Intensive agricultural research didn't begin in internationally-coordinated earnest until the Mexican government started encouraging the development of ways to increase crop yields to feed its booming population in the early 1940's.

This movement caught on in other developing countries, principally India, and ushered in the Green Revolution. It also increased dependence on petroleum-based fertilizers and monocultures, which are causing concern now. In any case, research into optimal soil mixtures and plant genetics continues apace, and every day we learn something more. Hey, maybe we'll find out from recent modern battlefields around the world that depleted uranium is just the thing to produce sugar-sweet ten-kilogram rutabagas. It could happen!

The Green Revolution refers to the dramatic increase in crop yields, particularly in cereal grains, that came about with advances in fertilizers, irrigation practices, and crop hybridization. This saved millions of people from the brink of starvation in the 1960's.

Right, so the question was: What is important? Well, imagine vegetable gardening as a graph. On the vertical axis, you have yield, and on the horizontal, there's money and effort. Fortunately, it takes little input to get a large amount of yield quickly. More input increases yield, but not as dramatically. For the purposes of this book, we're interested in finding that relevant minimum of what the soil needs to make the biggest difference in yield. Anything more increases expense, but doesn't give much more food for it. In other words, the time, effort and nutrients you put in should give you a decent "crop wage," that competes favorably with the effort and expense of going out to buy the same food, or, at least economically-speaking, it's not worth the trouble.

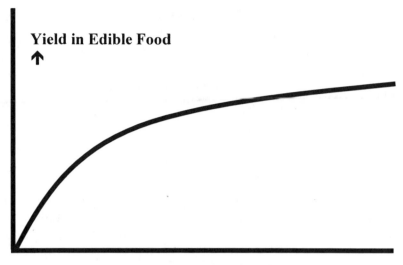

Yield in Edible Food ↑

Inputs: $$, Effort →

On that score, we know what the vast majority of vegetable plants need from the soil to produce an acceptable amount of food, though proportions vary depending upon the plant. The primary nutrients plants take up from their roots are nitrogen, phosphorus and potassium, usually in that order. Minerals secondary in importance are calcium, magnesium and sulfur. After that, plants need at least trace amounts of boron, chlorine, copper, iron, manganese, molybdenum and zinc. Plants also use some amount of carbon, hydrogen and oxygen, but unless you're growing a garden on a space station, they're readily available without any human intervention. Finally, the ability of plants to absorb this nutrition is contingent upon the acidity of the soil.

Nitrogen plays a big part in chlorophyll development, which is the pigment that makes plants green and where photosynthesis takes place, so it's clearly the most important element to plants. Nitrogen is all around us, being four-fifths of what we breathe, but plants and erosion deplete it from the soil pretty quickly. Even a casual gardener needs to be conscientious in ensuring sufficient nitrogen. Deprived plants usually develop yellow bottom leaves, which will travel up the plant if not corrected. Unfortunately, the soil can also have too much of a good thing. If the plants are a dark, leafy green and are slow to develop flowers and fruit, you're overdoing it.

Phosphorus is key to healthy root formation, flower and fruit production, and ripening.[19] Without phosphorus, photosynthesis is inhibited; the first compounds made in the photosynthetic reaction are triose phosphates. Plants in dire need of this mineral may be somewhat stunted, dark green with little or no fruit, and may even have a reddish-purplish cast to their stems and leaves. Plants really can't get enough phosphorus because it binds so readily and so tightly with other soil elements to make water insoluble compounds, which the plant can't access easily. For years, commercial farms poured phosphorus all over their fields with impunity. Waterways polluted with excess phosphorus see the growth of a lot of algae, which consumes the oxygen that fish need to breathe, resulting in mass die-offs. That's a problem.

> Those odd letters N, P and K, followed by numbers on the sides of commercial fertilizer packages stand for the chemical symbols of Nitrogen, Phosphorus and Potassium respectively. The numbers are their percentages by weight.

Potassium, a.k.a. potash, is needed for all-around good health and disease-resistance. Plants hurting for this stuff have yellow, "burned" spots on the leaves, crumpled leaves and some dead stems. Most plants aren't directly harmed by over-fertilization in potassium, but this mineral binds with magnesium, making magnesium then less available to the plant.

Nitrogen, Phosphorus and Potassium are the Big Three vital ingredients to healthy soil, and therefore healthy plants. Those other nine useful minerals are not nearly as vital and are generally present in sufficient quantities in all but the most unusual dirt[20], assuming the soil isn't just silt and sand. Whether or not certain minerals are sufficiently bio-available to the plant is a question of the soil's pH level.

---

[19] Bones are high in phosphorus. Ghoulish stories abound about early nineteenth century England digging up graves and battlefields in Europe to meet its voracious agricultural needs.

[20] Vegetable crops growing in the crags of granite rock will likely need boron supplements, for instance.

So what is pH and why is it important to the soil? The acronym pH stands for "potential of hydrogen," and it refers to the relative amounts of positively-charged hydrogen, H^+, atoms, versus negatively-charged hydroxide molecules, OH^-, in solution. A pH level of 7 is considered neutral, which means they're equal. A lower pH means more hydrogen, and is considered an acid. A higher pH means more hydroxide and that's a base, or alkaline.

> Have you ever heard the expression "sweeten the soil?" That means to make it more alkaline. Acids are considered "sour." This is easy to remember if you consider that wine and vinegar are acidic and sugar is basic. Bases are often bitter, too, like baking soda.

Right, you don't care. I didn't used to either, but I learned a little about it the hard way. Some time ago, I was musing about ways to get more compost in my garden before the big spring transplanting season, when I stumbled upon a county agency willing to deliver "half-finished" compost to my house for a small gasoline stipend. I was so excited, I didn't calculate out exactly what the "minimum twenty-five cubic yards" would look like in my driveway. The massive dump truck came the next day and covered over the two-car area, from the now-pushed-in garage door to the sidewalk, with a reeking, steaming pile of stick-infested black mire. It took me two months to spread this mess all over my front and back yards. When I was done, my whole property was easily six inches higher than it had been.

Half-finished compost tends to be acidic, but I was too desperate to reclaim some standing with my neighbors to worry about that as I hauled it to all my growing surfaces a wheelbarrow-load at a time. Shortly thereafter, I transplanted many of my garden window seedlings into the new soil. Quite by accident, I got a first-hand lesson in what acid soils will do to different plants.

The Bermuda grass in the front lawn was deliriously happy, springing out of the ground with deep-green vigor. The potatoes, blackberries, strawberries and artichokes joined in the raucous celebration. The tomatoes, pumpkins, onions and peppers were a little more uncertain, but before long they adjusted to their new pH level and put out impressive growth with reasonable fruit. That left the pole beans, cucumbers and basil. They looked faint within hours of transplant. By the next day, they'd visibly paled. I mixed in something near their roots to add base to the soil, and watered the poor things intensively for days, which finally saved the cukes and basil. The poor beans never quite recovered. Their color remained peaked and, though they did grow, their produce was sparse. Finally, aphids took advantage of their weakened state and that was the end of them.

Acid-Lovers (5.0-6.0):
  Potatoes
  Strawberries
  Pumpkins

Alkaline-Lovers:
  Brassicas, which include:
    Turnips
    Cauliflower
    Cabbage
    Broccoli
    Brussels Sprouts
but don't go higher than about 7.5.

So, what happened? The pH level affects the character of minerals in the soil, which affects their bioavailability. If it's too acid, for instance, many plants can't absorb nitrogen or phosphorus. But if it's too alkaline, metals like iron, manganese, boron, copper and zinc bind too tightly to other elements in the soil and are then no longer available to crops.

Different plants have different pH preferences. If you've got the time and want to create the perfect environment for each individual plant, or designate one of your garden plots for acid-lovers, and another for "alka-allies," knock yourself out. But I won't be deterred from my original mission, which is to instruct how to garden adequately with the least amount of time, effort and expense. And that is why I'm going to insist that though pH is an important consideration in soil, so long as yours is in the "sweet spot," at least 95% of your crops will do just fine. That "sweet spot" is actually slightly sour: 6.3-6.8. Check this once a year or so to make sure you're in the "zone," and then stop fretting about pH. If some pH tweaking is needed, read through the list of cheap or free sources of soil supplements below for what will sweeten or sour the soil, and try those first.

Great, but how do you check soil pH? Old-timers can actually taste the dirt and know if it's too sweet or sour, but I think I'll skip that method and go for the test kits and probes.

Soil test kits are readily available in garden centers and on-line, and even the cheap ones test more than just pH. Usually they can give readings on nitrogen, phosphorus and potassium, too. You can get years' worth of tests for less than twenty bucks, so they're well worth it.

Probes are even cheaper and last longer. They're just a metal stick you poke into wet ground to read the meter at the top. These are handy for spot checks. Just make sure the soil is truly wet, not just damp, or the reading will be off.

So, to review, sunlight is pretty much a constant. Water has to get to the plant in a timely manner, but it doesn't fundamentally change. Soil is a different animal altogether. It's constantly in a state of flux. Plants take more from soil than they put back directly, so without your due diligence in replacing what is lost, your garden production will suffer.

I also sense that most people reading this book will agree that growing your own food also has to provide a decent "wage;" that is, the expense of the undertaking must be sufficiently low compared to the return in order for the effort to be worthwhile. This book is not for the fussy hobbyist who has the time to milk-feed pumpkins and thin carrots with little scissors. We're busy, we're hungry and we're frugal.

Good news! The right soil doesn't have to come in little cubic-foot bags from the Prissy Plant Pavilion and cost more than the veggies grown in them. The trick is to let some stuff rot, then pour it on the garden. This carries the more dignified term of "composting." There's a whole chapter devoted to the mechanics of how to get it all to rot faster later. For now, just know that if you can make a pile, you can get lots of things for cheap or free which will build your soil very nicely, greatly reducing, or even eliminating the need to buy commercial soil-building materials. Below are some possible inputs to your compost heap:

Your now-spent vegetable plants robbed the soil in the first place. It seems only fair that you get at least some of the goods back from them. Once the crops are done for the season, rip them out and add them to the compost heap.

Weeds have much to be admired about them, believe it or not. They grow vigorously quite without the love and attention of anyone. They also provide much of what soil needs if they're composted, too. If you pull them up before they have a chance to flower, all is well. If they've had a chance to form seeds, your compost might not kill them. You could end up propagating more weeds later, so beware.

Kitchen scraps and some other garbage are wonderful soil boosters and carry the added advantages of diverting waste from landfills and cutting your garbage bill. Avoid meats and oil; they smell bad and attract critters.[21] But just about everything else is fair game, and rots amazingly quickly. Egg shells are good for calcium and they can sweeten soils. Coffee and tea grounds are good for adding acid. Even newspaper can be composted. Shred it, keep it wet and mix it well with other garbage.

Lye is a very caustic alkaloid used in many applications such as clearing drains, tanning hides and in making soap. It is made by draining water through wood ashes.

Human hair and bird feathers are each almost half nitrogen, and compost so well that some gardeners ask for the clippings from beauty salons.

Wood ashes provide some calcium and potassium and at least trace levels of almost all the other useful elements. They also raise soil pH, making it more alkaline. A little goes a long way. Note that the ashes need to be from actual wood. Ashes from other burnt things, including coal dust, aren't the same thing, and don't provide all of these benefits.

Lawn clippings rot quickly. They are great for nitrogen and other minerals. This will likely be a major component of your compost heap.

---

[21] I cheat and do add in fish scraps because they're so high in nitrogen, phosphorus and other nutrients for the soil. Remember the classic story of the Native Americans teaching the pilgrims how to grow corn (maize) by burying a fish with the seeds?

Leaves, especially the dried brown autumn harvest, provide carbon and trace elements. The roots of trees burrow down deep and bring up wonderful minerals, which they deposit in their leaves. High-nitrogen inputs to compost shrink down to practically nothing, but high-carbon material is the all-important "organic matter" that makes soil fluffy and workable,[22] holds water longer than sandy soil, breaks up clay soil; in short, it's the infrastructure, the medium for plants to grow in. Leaves will likely be another major component in your compost, and ultimately to your soil.

Straw provides much of what leaves do, except that leaves are probably better for some of the trace elements. Some gardeners use the bales to contain their compost piles, adding them in as they rot, too. If you can't get enough leaves, consider getting straw to provide some bulk to your garden soil.

Livestock manure is fabulous stuff for gardens. These are the concentrated remains of plants broken down already for easy incorporation into the soil, providing lots of nitrogen, phosphorous and potassium, as well as other minerals. Are there poultry farms, horse stables or dairies anywhere near where you live? They'll very likely give you as much as you can take, and more.

As for deer or other wild neighborhood herbivore scat, I couldn't find anywhere on the Internet raving about it. It's possible it contains too many weed seeds. Zoos often sell composted wild animal manure, so presumably just about any herbivore poop fertilizes well. Avoid dog and cat manure which not only aren't herbivorous, but are potentially harbor disease-causing bacteria. Sorry, Fido. The same goes for people manure.

Compost might be available for free from your local yard waste recycling site. I found out about this by first checking my garbage bill, which also collects the yard waste, then hopping on the website and noodling around until I saw something about compost delivery. One short phone call later, I was in business. In our county, they're desperate to get rid of the stuff, so they make you take a lot of it if you want it for free. Share with other gardeners if you can't work with the whole amount. As I mentioned earlier, if the compost is not completely rotted, it's likely acidic.

Bird and bat guano would be harder to collect, I imagine, but if

---

[22] That fluffy and workable quality to soil is also called "tilth" in garden books. It's just a short way of describing the ground's ability to be tilled.

you're near a cheap or free source, scrape some up.[23] If you have pet birds add their contributions, newspaper liner and all.

Aquarium water has nitrogen and other important nutrients for plants, so don't just dump it down your sink. There is more about how effective a fertilizer this is in Chapter Thirteen.

Seaweed was what the Irish used to rely on almost exclusively to fertilize their potato farms. While it doesn't provide huge amounts of the Big Three, it does have lots of trace elements. Its other advantage is that it breaks down quickly and therefore makes what it has available to the plants quickly. If you live near a beach, gather some and either mulch with it or toss it on the compost heap. Since the sea is salty, it wouldn't hurt to hose it off first.

Green manures are a misleading name because they aren't what most of us think of as manure at all. This is the practice of growing a nitrogen-fixing cover crop in between food crops. Good candidates are alfalfa, vetch, clover and buckwheat. The trick is to let the crop

A good, cheap way to get seed for a green manure crop is to buy a big bag of birdseed. It's a good mix of legumes and grasses.

grow until a time before it flowers and goes to seed, then turn it under your soil. Because it's got so much nitrogen, it rots into the ground in just a few weeks, replenishing the soil nicely, after which you can plant your next food crop. This is not strictly free for the home gardener, as you'd have to buy the seed, but if bought in bulk it should be well worth the expense.

Urine, unlike human poop,[24] is sterile when it leaves the body,[25] though it can pick up microorganisms once outside. If you're careful collecting it, urine is excellent fertilizer for the home garden. Be sure to pour it on your compost pile the same day it's collected, or it will start to convert to ammonia, which smells. It's a fantastic source of

[23] While doing research, I came across a product called "Mosquito and Gnat Scat Granules," and thought at first that someone had actually gone to the trouble of collecting the feces of these tiny insects for a garden product! On closer inspection, however, the granules turn out to have all-natural, aromatic ingredients that *repel* the insects. Oh, *that* "scat."
[24] Human poop is also known as night soil. An appalling number of countries allow its use in agriculture, resulting in all-too-frequent bacterial outbreaks.
[25] Don't use urine from people with urinary tract infections, as it will not be sterile.

the Big Three primary elements plants need, as well as some trace minerals. Urine even beats commercial fertilizers in effectiveness. So good is this stuff that I've read that a man could grow enough grain to feed himself with just the nutrients that his urine provides. If it's good enough for NASA's hydroponics experiments, it's good enough for us.

To be on the cautious side, don't use urine directly in the garden for a couple of weeks before the harvest, but if you want to fertilize with it, just dilute it about three-to-one with water first to avoid "burning" plants with the acid content. You can put this solution in a spray bottle and apply it directly to the leaves of your plants, too. Urine does contain salt, how much depends on your intake, so stay away from the potato chips. Also, don't fertilize the same area too much with urine at a time. The salts could build up faster than other forces can dissolve them.

Urine had many uses in Colonial Times.

- As a solvent for tanning leather
- By dyers for fixing color
- As a bleach
- It's a chief ingredient in saltpeter, which is a key component in gunpowder
- As crop fertilizer, of course

For those of you who are asking: yes, golden elixir from your dog would work, too. The problem comes with the logistical issue of collection. I'd love to hear from readers who successfully trained Rex to aim at a container.

If you're still cringing at the very thought of using human urine to fertilize your vegetable garden, consider the water savings from fewer flushes. There's even the argument that less nitrogen in sewage means less pollution in our waterways. And, if you get your supply from your sons, you'll also likely find that your bathrooms stay cleaner. If that doesn't clinch it for you...

So there you have it; fifteen different sources of very cheap or free soil components, at least half of which even an urban, rooftop gardener can easily obtain. If you're conscientious about seeing the possibilities in the materials around you, the effort to toss them on your compost heap is certainly much less than grabbing the keys and hauling back pricey bags of peat moss and chelated iron from your local nursery.

Sun. Water. Soil. If these are in place, the garden makes dinner for even the laziest person. Keep the soil thriving and the plants will take care of the rest, providing you with fresh, wholesome food for the entire growing season.

Chapter Five
Don't Be a Tool

The famous economist Milton Friedman once said, "The problem of social organization is how to set up an arrangement under which greed will do the least harm; capitalism is that kind of a system." [26] He may be on to something. Certainly, as socialism and communism try to remove personal gain from their plans, they also remove incentive, and it's not long until the economy collapses. Capitalism works, albeit imperfectly, because it doesn't attempt to deny man's baser nature of self-interest.

But that doesn't mean greed doesn't cause any harm. You sometimes see its effects in advertising. It's not enough to tout how delicious the cookies are; some ads try to instill insecurity into anyone who would consider not buying the cookies. Don't you love your children? Don't you *deserve* this treat? Aren't you a *smart* shopper? Such is the pressure in buying gardening gadgets. Every single one of them claims to be the one true necessity for perfect vegetables. You can blow quite a wad on all of this stuff. I made the mistake once of browsing a catalog and became positively infatuated with a device that promised superior tomatoes because you could

---

[26] The economist Adam Smith said essentially the same thing two centuries earlier, but his treatise on capitalism, *The Wealth of Nations* is such a mule-choker, no one but Ph.D. candidates gets through the whole thing.

grow them *upside-down*. What a perfectly high maintenance boondoggle! Still, I was ready to fill out that order form. Only at the last minute did I come to my senses.

While tomatoes are perfectly capable of growing well right side up during the summer, there is logic to pulling them out and hanging them upside down before the first frost. This is to encourage the ripening of those last green tomatoes for Thanksgiving.

The question, as always, boils down to what's important, and what isn't. The important tools work with the important elements in growing food, which are climate, water and the nutrients, i.e. dirt.

Supplies important from a climate perspective generally fall under the auspices of protection. By blunting climate extremes for the plants, you can extend their growing and harvesting time. **Row covers**, for instance, let in light and moisture, but keep plants warmer longer, delaying frost damage. **Cold frames** are more durable structures, basically boxes with transparent glass or plastic on top to keep cold, frost and snow at bay and extend the harvest. **Greenhouses**, both the tent-like and more permanent, do the same thing. Even putting a **milk carton** over a seedling helps to protect it from the elements.

The principle of making a more hospitable micro-climate around your plants is very simple, and so can the materials be to accomplish the goal. One year, our newspapers came in transparent red plastic bags. I'd read somewhere that tomatoes liked red light, so I used them over some of the seedlings, which worked just fine, as long as I remembered to make a few small holes in the bags to let them breathe. We kept our orange tree from the worst of the frost damage during one freak cold snap by simply draping it with old bath towels overnight. One of my kids got special "Mommy Time" by helping me hammer simple frames together from scrap wood and stapling plastic sheeting over them so I could put my pepper plants outside a month early. Carrot seeds are notoriously difficult to sprout unless kept constantly moist, a feat best accomplished with a clear plastic cover right on the soil. You can see if it needs more water; otherwise just leave it in place until the seedlings push up against it. Don't buy clear plastic; use it from all the packaging that comes with products you buy anyway. Look around at what's available first and see if you can make something work before shelling out for the patented "Extendo-Season 9000."

Supplies to deliver water to plants don't have to be expensive, either. It's often more economical to buy long **garden hoses**, then cut them down to the size you want for your purposes. You can buy new ends for the hoses separately and rather inexpensively to "make" the new hoses. The same goes for repair kits to fix holes in hoses. For leaks at the junctions, a new rubber washer tucked inside the female end of the hose, and/or plumber's tape, mentioned in Chapter Three, usually takes care of the problem.

I already went into long detail about **drip systems**. If that's the direction you want to go, you can buy just the components you need, like large coils of quarter-inch tubing or a bulk package of emitters inexpensively, for repairs or expansions.

Splitters that attach to faucets to create more than one head on which to attach hoses are awfully convenient. Not only do they let you keep something semi-permanently attached to one side of the faucet, but they allow the flow of water in that direction to be shut off manually, without disabling the whole water source. Spray attachments to hoses are also handy. They control the flow of the water, often giving you several different types of sprays, and they save water by shutting off when the trigger isn't pulled. Make sure that you have some way to effect a gentle spray, either from a watering can or a spray attachment; you need something to water small seeds that could easily be washed away if the water flow is too powerful.

Supplies for working in the dirt and compost pile are legion, but really you don't need much more than a few tools to:

- Turn dirt over

- Move dirt from one place to the other

- Even the dirt out in the plot

- Deal with weeds

- Make small holes for transplanting

- Protect your hands

For turning dirt over, nothing beats a **garden fork**. This looks like the illicit love child of a pitchfork and a shovel; they have four or so tines like a pitchfork, but those tines are fat, giving it a more shovel-like behavior in the dirt. In digging up stubborn ground, the tines travel through the earth much more readily than a shovel, saving you some backache.

I should mention that established gardens don't require a lot of digging each year. Once good soil is in place, earthworms do the job of keeping the soil aerated and non-compacted, so disrupting them with your own digging can do more harm than good. Deep digging also brings dormant weed seeds to the surface where the sunlight can wake them up. Just add your new soil to the top, stir it in shallowly, and let the worms do the rest. In my case, I don't know any other way to get rid of the long runners of Bermuda grass that want to take over the planet, than to reach down with my garden fork and rip the roots up to the surface. Most other young weeds are more shallow.

To move dirt from one place to another, there are short-distance and long-distance solutions. For a short distance, the classic **shovel** is still the way to go. Longer distances are easier with a **wheelbarrow** or four-wheeled dump cart.

Simple **rakes**, especially those with strong metal tines do a great job of smoothing out dirt before planting. You'll save water if it flows over the surface evenly. The rakes with flimsier tines are helpful for gathering leaves, but if you can only afford one, the less-yielding rake will do.

There are a number of devices to deal with weeds. The **hoe** is a classic; but again, if you're short on start-up funds, just dig the weeds up with a shallow scrape of your shovel. Or reach down and pull them up yourself.

Transplanting is down-in-the-dirt work. Anything that can scoop to make a hole for the new tenant will work. The **hand spade,** also known as a **trowel** is expected tool here, but old forks and spoons from thrift stores cost only pennies and work almost as well. I didn't mention the need for pots in which to start seedlings; just about any container that can hold dirt and let excess water drain will work, which encompasses everything from eggshells to yogurt cups, to old coffee cans. Your plants will not care one way or the other if they started out life in a cardboard egg carton, or a professional-looking water-expanded disk of peat moss and "growing medium," whatever that is. Use your imagination for finding containers for starting seeds. My husband once brought home some heavy-duty plastic pieces used to hold large computers away from the sides of the crate during shipping. They have a cup shape with a hole in the bottom. As well-trained as he is, Hubby immediately saw the gardening possibilities.

Heavy-duty **gloves** primarily do the job of protecting you from splinters and blisters from the handles of your tools. Then there are "garden gloves," which are light protection mostly for keeping dirt out from under your fingernails. Half the time, I start off with the garden gloves, then end up taking them off because I can't feel what I'm doing, so I just scrub off my hands as best as I can afterwards with a brush.

Growing your own food doesn't require a large amount of capital outlay. Rototillers are not only expensive to buy and maintain, but they chew through highly-beneficial earthworms. They also actually compact the soil beneath the blades over time, making it hard for roots to go deep and save you water.

Chippers and shredders are nice for speeding up composting, but there are workarounds. You can run over things with a lawn mower to shred them. Machetes and electric trimmers can help, too.

If I had to put a number on the rock-bottom amount of capital outlay needed to start a garden, I'd say $50 would be enough for at least the garden fork, a cheap hose, and some seeds. For $100, you could buy most of the remaining necessary tools. Double that again for your drip system and a few conveniences. That $200 may sound like a lot, but you can grow enough food to pay for it in your first year.

Part II
The Growing Year

There's an old Chinese folktale I read once of a little peasant boy meeting a proud warrior who rides tall astride his muscular steed. If I remember how it goes, said warrior tarries the boy at a fork in the road to ask the direction to Beijing. The boy points to his right, whereupon the warrior thanks him and starts to gallop away in the opposite direction. The boy shouts after him that he's going the wrong way, but the warrior replies, "That's all right, this is a very fast horse."

This section of the book is all about getting your garden to go in the direction of greater yield for minimal work. Part I was the "thinking" section, where a would-be gardener first considers what plants really need, something of their likes and dislikes, what they enjoy doing for fun, and so forth. Now we take the information from the first part and finally do some actual work, toward where Part I was pointing.

Even if your area has a short growing season, there is work you can spread out through the course of the year, which decrease the overall amount of labor you have to put into the garden. Yield will increase, as the soil

will be fertile well in advance of the needs of the plants.

Some gardeners are like the proud warrior with the fast horse. They'll have to work a lot harder and buy a lot more because they didn't consider the easier path to a productive garden. Instead, consider the much simpler inputs that a garden needs throughout the year, sort of like the simple peasant boy who makes his leisurely way to the capitol.

Chapter Six
Fall: Leaf It Be

The fliers in the newspaper and commercials on television only advertise garden supplies in the spring, but the real beginning of the grower's year is in the autumn. If you start in the spring, you'll have starved your dirt all winter long, and you'll only be able to keep your plants alive with regular infusions of expensive commercial fertilizers.

Fall has an official start date of around September 21, when I use the term, it's a bit more amorphous because it depends on your climate. The "autumn" for our purposes is that time when the warm-season vegetables are giving up production and even starting to die back. For some areas, that autumn begins before the calendar autumn. In Zone Nine, we can often leave our tomatoes

Fall Task List:

- Pull out old plants
- Save seed
- Put beds "to bed"
- Start winter crops
- Extend the harvest with covers
- Plan for next year

and basil to their own devices or with light night cover until mid-November.

The first job for the autumn is to rip out all the plants that have done their time. Before you add them to the newest compost heap, check for any overripe vegetables that can yield seed for next year. Bring those vegetables into the house, cut them open, and dry the seeds on a paper towel until completely dry. Store them in the refrigerator or other cool, dry place until next year. If you're good about this, you won't need to buy new seed for beans, tomatoes, squashes, melons, peppers, cucumbers ...

If you have a drip system, drain the lines as best as you can, then coil them up and store them somewhere, preferably out of the elements. Even if you're growing winter vegetables, which we'll discuss later, there's usually enough dew and rain to meet their watering needs. Rake to even out the soil and fill up cavities left from the pulled up plants.

Another excellent autumn task is to start new garden plots, if you can. Punch down through the sod with your garden fork, then turn it over and let it rot back into your soil. Once you've done this for the whole new bed, decide whether or not you want to border it. There are a few advantages to doing this:

- The border keeps some weeds from creeping into your plot.

- The whole plot is level, rather than mounded, which is better for watering purposes.

- Bordered plots can hold more workable dirt because they're raised slightly.

- Raised beds warm faster than the surrounding ground in the spring.

- They look better.

The disadvantage is in some initial work and expense to acquire materials and make the border. Arguably, digging around the border is also more difficult than if there were no obstacle at all.

In all the plots that won't be growing anything until spring, and that includes the plot(s) you just started, this is the time to lay those soil-builders on thick. Earthworms and composting bacteria will have all autumn and winter under the nice, warm cover you provide to break up materials and incorporate the nutrients into the ground. Come spring, you'll have soft, workable, fertile dirt; a feast for vegetable plants.

So, what breaks down fast on the ground? Leaves. Gather every last leaf from the whole neighborhood if you can and dump them onto your plots; a foot deep isn't too much. Water thoroughly to keep them from blowing away, and to start the moisture's work on turning those leaves to mush. Until the rains come, make sure this doesn't dry out completely. Some gardeners like to cover the whole thing with newspaper or plastic to keep it even warmer. In areas with heavy snow, that might be good; you want to encourage earthworms and bacteria to do what they do best, which is to recycle dead stuff back into nutrients for the soil. Just make sure the cover can breathe and let in moisture. Now leave these plots alone until you're ready to use them in the spring. I call this "putting the beds to bed." This is a bit of a misnomer, since they won't be hibernating at all.

Spreading leaves on the plots isn't exactly "composting" in the classic sense of the word. True aerobic composting, with lots of nitrogen involved, could starve the soil of oxygen and kill your worms, so this high-carbon material makes "leaf mold." All the wonderful organic material and nutrients from the leaves will build more tilth and water-retaining properties into the dirt. In short, this is a soil-building exercise. There'll be more on composting in Chapter Ten.

Some of your crops still have produce on them that isn't quite ripe. If you want to encourage the ripening process, keep them warmer as the weather starts to turn, especially those plunging temperatures at night. Sure, moving them into a heated greenhouse would be nice, but most of us don't have the funds for that. Now would be the time to break out those simple row covers and make sure the plants are tucked into them at night. Just this simple step stretches the harvest season somewhat.

Some gardeners get salads and root crops all winter long by keeping the cold and snow away with cold frames. Run an Internet search and you'll find all kinds of clever plans for these from enthusiastic engineers who also garden, In reality, a cold frame can be something as simple as four hay bales with the pane of an old storm window on top. Build it around something you want to eat for longer.

Can you plant even now? Well, that depends on your USDA Hardiness Zone, discussed in detail in Chapter Two. If the ground doesn't freeze solid, you should be able to extend the harvest for some crops by the methods already described above, but there also has to be adequate sunlight to encourage actual growing, and not every Zone can make it work. Serious gardeners will quibble with me on this one, but I doubt it's worth all the effort for any Zone lower than 8, and even 8 has to be pretty intentional about cold frames or an unheated greenhouse to pull it off. See Appendix A for a list of cool-season vegetables to try. I can't recommend a winter garden, planted in the autumn, enough!

> Need old storm windows? Call your local window installer. They often remove old windows before installing new ones, and have to dispose of them. They're usually more than happy to let you haul some away.

- Most root crops, such as carrots, turnips, radishes and parsnips, are sweeter and altogether better-tasting in the winter.

- Store-bought salad is so expensive this time a year, but yours isn't!

- Most pests are hibernating.

- A winter garden needs practically no water.

- Your family is eating fresh, healthy food while everyone else's is shipped from the other hemisphere.

Regardless of your USDA Zone, even in the dead of winter, you can grow sprouts indoors. It's great to have something fresh and green for salads and sandwiches, and it couldn't be easier to do. There's a clear jar. There's a lid for that jar that can drain water while keeping seeds and sprouts from pouring out. Finally, you need seeds for sprouting. I'm not going too fast, am I?

Now put the seeds in the jar and cover with water for a few hours or overnight. Rinse the seeds and drain out the water. Put the jar somewhere where sun won't get to it, like a closet or in a thick paper bag. Once a day, rinse the seeds and drain the water again to keep them moist and mold-free. Once the seeds have sprouted and grown maybe half an inch, put them in a sunny windowsill. Don't forget to rinse them every day! Once they're green, they're good to eat. You can keep them for a few days in the refrigerator at that point; just don't let them dry out.

Fall is mainly the "housekeeping" season; out with the old, get ready for the new. It might be tempting to skip some of these chores, but that would be a mistake. By feeding the beds now, the ground does all the work of packing itself with nutrients over the cold months. Come spring and summer, you can concentrate your energies on actually growing the food,

Sprouts to try:

- Alfalfa
- Broccoli
- Red Clover
- Lentils
- Mung Bean
- Oats
- Radish
- Soybean
- Wheat

Check health food stores for seeds and more information.

effectively halving the amount of work and more than that of the expense involved in vegetable gardening.

Chapter Seven
Winter: The Need for Seed

Ah, distinctly I remember it was in the bleak December,
And each separate dying ember
wrought its ghost upon the floor.
Eagerly I wished the morrow; - vainly I had sought
to borrow
From my books surcease of sorrow - sorrow for the lost ... "[27]

Sweet corn? Ah, buck up. Even in the dark days of winter, there is something constructive to do for the garden. For one thing, after those dying embers are done wreaking their ghosts wherever, you're saving them for soil sweetener, right?

Wintertime is the time to make plans! Since those plans are best if they are informed by experience, and that

Winter Task List:

- Update notes
- Decide the crops for next year
- Buy seeds
- Start seedlings

---

[27] This is part of the second stanza of Edgar Allan Poe's *The Raven*, 1845. As in, "Quoth the raven, 'Nevermore.'"

experience is founded on memory, now is a good time to talk about keeping notes throughout the year for the garden.

Basically, you're trying to chronicle what worked, when it worked, what you did with what worked and what didn't work. I recommend a three-ring binder for this information, and here's why: I tend to lose my dumb garden notebook, sometimes for days at a time. If I'm using an all-in-one book for this, then I can't make notes for days on end. But if it's in a binder, I find any old scrap of paper to scribble on and add it to the notebook when it turns up again. You could argue that I could just lose the loose papers, too, but I have a place for those. It's the notebook I misplace because sometimes I take it to the office, or the living room, or the garden shed, or the family room, or even in bed before I turn in. So, when inevitably it disappears, I just go about my life, and when the notebook resurfaces, I add the pages I've made since the last time I lost it. Working around my flaws is just easier than expecting perfection.

At the very least, a garden notebook should keep track of the following information:

- Plant varieties grown

- When a planting was started

- Harvest dates

A bare bones note system might look graphically something like this:

	January	February	March	April
apples	—			
artichokes	▓			▓
basil	skipped this year			
beets				
blackberries				
broccoli	▓	▓	▓	▓
cabbage			▓	▓
carrots			▓	
celery		cutting celery		
chard	▓	▓	▓	▓
corn			▓	▓
cucumbers			▓	▓
garlic	▓	▓	▓	▓
green beans			▓	▓

In this example, the lightly shaded areas indicate harvest availability. The darker blocks denote when the crop was planted. For space considerations, this is only four months out of a chart that could stretch to encompass the whole year. At a glance, you can see basically what you grew, though the actual variety would be helpful to know elsewhere. The dark shading corresponds to where new seeds started, and the light shade shows the harvest time. What can you do with this information?

- Take note of the length of harvest and see if it can be extended the following year, in either or both calendar directions.

- Note the gaps in harvest to determine how often you need to replant some crops to ensure continuous harvest.

- Know what is ripe right now for meal-planning purposes.

- Determine your seed shopping list.

- With this list of what you can grow, and when, you can plan where to plant specific vegetables into your plots.

A more detailed system should include as much weather information as you can gather.

- Daily, or weekly high/low temperatures

- Comparison with regional average high/low temperatures

- If rain or snow, gauge amount

Don't leave out any information on what methods you used in cultivation.

- If there is a crop failure, note why.

- If you tried covers or cold frames, describe how they worked and on what plants.

- Make careful note of what varieties of vegetables you grew and how they fared in the garden; you think you'll remember, but you won't!

- If you used special fertilizers or treatments, write it down.

- Note when pH readings taken, and what they were, and what you did to rectify any imbalances.

- Any pests? Write down the pest, how you treated it, and if it worked.

- It doesn't hurt to keep a diary of your investment and returns, either.

- How much time does the garden require from you every week?

- What tasks did you do?

- How much water are you using, and how much does it cost?

- How much money did you spend on supplies?

- Did you learn how to get better yields from particular plants?

- How much did you harvest from each plant, and how many meals did that make?

- How many plants in a specific crop do you need to adequately provide for your family's needs?

- How much do the same vegetables cost at the store at the same time you're harvesting yours? This is good for quantifying your savings and determining your true "hourly wage."

Obviously, the drawback to all this is that it takes time to gather this data. Gauge for yourself how much of it is important to you, and record accordingly. Develop some kind of system to make the reports highly readable and easy to consult. This is not a diary; you want something formulaic so it can be consulted quickly. In the winter, you hopefully have time to compile some of this material into a cohesive report that will help you strategize for the next growing season.

So, what is there to think about when planning for the warmer weather? Basically, you want to know how much to plant, where to plant it, how often to plant it, and when. Draw a diagram as close to scale as possible of your garden spaces and mark with numbers corresponding to where you want to put the cool-season plants first. If you took good notes from the previous year, you'll already have an inkling about how much space you'll need for them, otherwise hazard your best guess.

Using those same numbers, move on to the warmer-season plants that will grow in the same spaces later. Repeat if you can cram in a still later-season crop after that; we Zone Niners sometimes can. Here's an example. Modify this for your own needs:

South West Plot, 4 X 8'

1. Garlic and snap peas | pole beans w/ corn and pumpkins | lettuce mix and spinach
2. Lettuce and spinach mix | tomatoes and carrots | onions
3. Onions | onions and basil | snap peas
4. Turnips, carrots and garlic | peppers | garlic

In this simple diagram, note that snap peas, lettuce and spinach, onions and various root crops will all be cultivated first, since they'll enjoy the cooler season.

After they quit, transplant in the plants for your warmest season. If there will be enough time before snow, take advantage of the cooling weather to get in another planting that can still be harvested after light frosts.

This plan can be as simple or as complicated as you'd like. The purpose in working this out ahead of time is simply to:

- ensure all the food you want to grow actually has a place, and

- that everything you want to eat will be available when the weather will cooperate.

If you plan ahead, all you have to do is to consult your notebook later; very little thinking needs to be done when you're laboring outside in the sun.

Once some sort of stratagem is in place, wintertime is also the perfect time to lay in the supplies that will be needed to bring it into fruition…literally! Make a list of what is needed.

- Seeds
- Tools
- Drip system parts, if applicable

The other nice thing about shopping for your garden supplies in the winter is that you have the time to shop for bargains. One caution: some seeds can be difficult to order for delivery before spring. A lot of mail-order seed companies are located in the East, where they're buried under blizzards until May. I have a hard time getting them to send me my tomato seeds in time to start them indoors right after the New Year. Consider this challenge another argument in favor of saving your own seed.

We're aiming to have as much fresh food for as much of the year as possible, so winter time is also a great time to get a jump on the spring by starting seedlings indoors.

What should you start indoors? Good candidates are anything that can grow outdoors in the season to come, and even some slower growing plants for later, that you intend to repot before you transplant. Bear in mind though, that some plants don't transplant well. Appendix A makes note of those for your convenience. Sadly, many of them are cool-season plants like lettuce and root crops. Snap peas and broccoli are fair game, though!

How much time ahead of the good planting weather should you start your seedlings? Read the back of the seed packets for germination times; that's your first clue. Then, based on the packet's stated length of time until the plant will produce, figure you can safely keep the plant indoors for about a sixth of that time after germination. This is also assuming that your pot is big enough to give the roots plenty of room.

Vegetable gardening is a year-round commitment, so it's fair to revisit the question of effort versus reward. Will the food ultimately be worth the work? I say "yes" for the following reasons:

- Moving some of the work to the "off-season" evens out the labor so the burden isn't concentrated in the growing season.

- Dumping soil-building ingredients into the beds and leaving them to break down by themselves is much less work than regular, expensive infusions of commercial fertilizer later.

- Planning the garden on paper saves time and avoids mistakes later.

- Acquiring the supplies you'll need for the coming year, much of which you can just order on-line from the comfort of your office and have shipped to you, avoids costly delays during the growing season that could result in gaps in your food supply.

- Starting early takes no more effort overall than starting later, but results in more food for a longer part of the year.

That last point is what you're really going to appreciate when the spring planting arrives.

Chapter Eight
Spring: The Plot Thickens

In the book *The Lion, The Witch and the Wardrobe*, the reader instantly understands that it's the beginning of the end of winter when Father Christmas at last penetrates Narnia. And though the White Witch loses nothing of her frosty malevolence, the snow gets wetter and green things begin to appear. The long-awaited true ruler of Narnia, Aslan, is coming and with him, spring.[28]

Likewise, by degrees, some almost too subtle to notice, winter begins to lose its hold on your backyard. I notice it when the skiing up in the mountains becomes slower going and less maneuverable, due to the heavier, wetter snow. I usually quit for the season about then to save my knees. The twigs on fruit trees develop little "muscles" bulging with buds. Some of the birds are back. Is it time to "wake up" the garden?

Spring Task List:

- Uncover beds
- Transplant seedlings
- Start seedlings
- Grow green manures
- Update notes

---

[28] C.S. Lewis, 1950.

Run an Internet search on "last frost date" and you'll find several sites that can give you a rough idea when you can expect that your less-hardy cool-season vegetables can safely come outside. However, no one can be absolutely certain the White Witch doesn't have at least one last sucker punch in her before she succumbs to spring. If you're anxious to get the garden going, put out a few of your plants, then a few more each week for the next couple of weeks until it's obvious winter is truly gone.

As far as you can tell, nothing's happened in those garden plots the last few months, but get out your rake for a closer inspection. The leaves and other big pieces still dominate the top, but one you brush away that thin crust, notice how nice the dirt looks. For now, scoop those large pieces out of the garden and put them back in the compost pile. The slugs and snails will be out in force soon and we don't need to give them any safe passage through the wet leaves to our plants. There will be more on how to deal with them in Chapter Sixteen. Once the covering is gone, you should have fresh, dark soil, perfect for welcoming your "little ones" into the world, be they seeds or seedlings. Add some finished compost now, and mix it in a bit, for added fertility. You can check the soil pH; it will likely be right where you want it. Do leave the beds covered until there are plants to go into them, to get as much nutrition into the soil and to discourage weeds from sprouting.

I found useful "last frost date" data compiled by the government at:

http://cdo.ncdc.noaa.gov/cgi-bin/climatenormals/climatenormals.pl?directive=prod_select2&prodtype=CLIM2001&subrnum%20to%20Freeze/Frost%20Data%20from%20the%20U.S.%20Climate%20Normals

The seedlings have had an easy life up until now and aren't ready for the harsh new reality of outdoor living. Don't blame yourself. You just wanted them to have every privilege you never had, and before you knew it, they'd become spoiled. Now you have to get them used to the new outdoor paradigm or they won't thrive. This is called "hardening off." It's a bit like "tough love" for plants. Start by setting the plants outside to soak up the mid-day sun for a couple of hours, then gradually lengthen the exposure for a few days. Even after you stick them in the ground, it won't hurt to cover them for a night or two.

Transplant carefully, or the plants will suffer damage, which will inhibit yield down the line, or kill them outright. The strongest part of most plants is the stem, so hold that part, and the dirt around it, turn the container upside down and gently slide the plant and all the dirt out. If the stem is too fragile, you may need to use a hand spade or spoon to scoop the plant and all its delicate roots out of the container. Don't tear them! If you do, you'll stunt the plant. Keep at least some of the original container dirt around the plant so the roots are protected in the new space.

It's about this time of the year that you'll notice your neighbors are all spending copious amounts of time furiously digging, weeding and fertilizing their plots. Try not to feel left out of all the fun. You won't have much in the way of weeds because your plots were covered through the cold season. The cover also provided a good deal of fertilizer in the process. And because you kept the earthworms busy, your soil will be nice and soft, too. In fact, the less you disrupt the ground, the happier our highly beneficial worms will be and the fewer weed seeds you'll expose to the sun. See? You're not lazy, you're smart.

Or you're lazy *and* smart … and well-fed.

If you want to turbo-charge your soil, and you aren't using all your "acreage" for cool-season crops, then now would be a good time to consider a green manure crop, especially before introducing a heavy-feeding warm-season planting, like corn. Green manures got more mention in Chapter Four. All you're doing is letting this crop grow for just a couple of weeks or so then turning it under and letting it rot a few more weeks to bring nitrogen and other good stuff into the ground. Uncover your plot, and sprinkle your seeds on the soil right before rain is expected. The rain will both water and "plant" the seeds, making less work for you. You could have done this toward the end of the summer, but I find this harder for a few reasons:

- I seldom have the space at that point, since this is right at the juncture of the warm-season and cool-season plot occupations.
- Nitrogen leaches so readily out of soil that doesn't have a lot

of carbon in it to keep there, which is what the leaves provide.

- In my area, there isn't enough rain at that time of year to make this a low-maintenance job.

To be fair, most green manures will sprout more readily in the waning summer than they will over the gathering spring, but if weeds can do it, so can your green manure, eventually.

Springtime shouldn't be about preparing the soil. It's about getting the food plants into the ground. Try to designate at least a half-hour each week to start or transplant something. If you're transplanting, also take the time to make sure the water will be there when you need it. If that's a drip system, put the hoses and emitters, or little sprinklers if you've got seedlings, right where the plants will need them. At this point, you might still be getting enough rain or dew that you're not concerned about sufficient water yet, but don't wait until the plants get larger and it gets harder to get the hoses in place.

With each new seed start, jot the date in your notebook. Consider multiple plantings of some of the same crop if you want continuous availability throughout the harvesting time. Appendix A contains some advice on which crops have an especially short harvest. From mid-spring or so, plant your warm-season seeds indoors so they'll be ready for transplanting just as soon as the "first stringers" overheat.

Once you've got plants in the ground, there isn't much to do but wait for something to eat. Luckily, most of the cool-season crops are speedy in that regard. You'll have salad greens and the radishes to go with them in a small number of weeks. Other root crops and snap peas won't be too far behind. Broccoli and cabbage might lag a bit, but they'll be along soon.

If you're diligent about always having something new ready to replace something spent, you can have a continuous supply of food right up until your first hard frost in the autumn. The time investment for this is only twenty minutes or so every few days, less time than you'd spend thumping and sniffing prospective vegetable purchases at the grocery store. I can't emphasize this point enough. If you let nature and the plants do most of the work, then you can grow nutritious, money-saving food while still having a life!

Chapter Nine
Summer: The Livin' Is Easy

The first house my husband and I bought was in a really dicey neighborhood, but we were so happy to be able to buy anything anywhere, we didn't consider the three most important things in real estate. Any agent will tell you that these are: location, location and location.

How bad was it? Well, in the five years we lived there, we were frequently panhandled, even by neighbors. The kids down the street had a pretty steady drug

Summer Task List:

- Transplant seedlings
- Start seeds outside
- Update notes

operation going on at the corner, which occasionally made someone really mad. Once, after a drive-by shooting, we picked ourselves off of the floor and found shell casings on the ground in front of our house. There was also an insurance fire, a car crash, something thrown through our window, gunfire many evenings, police helicopters circling overhead …just another beautiful day in the neighborhood!

So, the morning we headed out our front door to go to work and found police surrounding our place, guns drawn, we weren't exactly surprised. *Attentive* might be a better word for it. Just as if we'd been doing this all our lives, (and by that point we were beginning to think we had), we cautiously stepped outside, hands high in the air and waited for instructions.

At first, it was if the police didn't even see us. So we ventured a couple of steps forward. Still nothing. After a couple more steps and no reaction from the guys in blue, we were close enough to address someone and inquire, *politely*, as to the nature of their visit?

We must have looked pretty silly because as grim as he seemed in those no-nonsense mirrored dark glasses, crouching low behind his car, one of the cops couldn't help but smile and straighten up a little. He explained that the nice boys who'd just moved in next door were running a chop shop for stolen cars. They were guarding our place as a precaution to prevent a backyard escape.

With that, they let our car out of the driveway, and we headed off to another day at the office. We used to work late a lot back then.

Gardening in the summer is kinda like my old neighborhood. I don't like to go outside when it's just too hot.

As luck would have it, very little labor is required in the garden during the hot part of the year, *if*(!) the plants are getting adequate water. Skimp or just get irregular with this, and your harvest will suffer.

Part of the whole water supply issue is to retain it, of course. Remember the leaves you raked away in the spring? Put them back on the soil now, right up to the base of your plants. On a drip system, you can even cover all the emitters and hoses. This mulch will slow evaporation and even keep the ground cooler, which a lot of plants will appreciate if your high temperatures reach cookie-baking levels.

The same rules apply for summer as for spring: Keep replacing the old with the new in order to have a steady supply of food. The only difference in the summer is that you should add in an inch or so of compost between plantings to keep the soil rich.

It's up to you if you want to start seeds indoors. On the one hand, you'll be able to grow more simultaneously, thereby cutting the time from planting in the garden to the harvest. On the other hand, seeds directly in the soil at this point sprout and grow pretty quickly in the warmth, so if you're low on time, you can probably still have enough food if you avoid the chore of transplanting for a bit.

That transition in the harvest from the cool-season vegetables to the new crops is like Christmas all over again. Just when you start to get tired of all the stews, stir fries and green salads, along come the pastas, pestos and grilling veggies. Really, this hottest part of the growing season is the big payoff for all the work you did the previous seasons. The main job you have now is to bring the harvest in. It's so much fun to go out early every morning with a basket to pick the day's fruits and veggies.

Sit back, drink some mint tea, and enjoy all that ripe, delicious food coming your way.

Part III
More with Less Work

Hubby and I once painted the whole outside of our house. It took a solid three weeks, many sore muscles and other minor injuries, and

lots and lots of cursing to get it looking more or less right.

Years later, our latest house needed painting. Hubby suggested I break out the ladders; I suggested he sleep in the garage. So we hired a professional, who got the whole thing done in a couple of days.

So what made the difference between a couple of paint-splattered homeowners and the pro? He had the benefit of a few tools, yes, but the main thing was pure skill and applied knowledge.

Part I covered the foundational implements to growing food. Part II encompassed what the year basically entails for the gardener who's in it for the food, and only the food. And now we've come to Part III.

Part III is about some of those tools, skills and applied knowledge that make gardening even easier and cheaper. You still won't be a "professional," but you'll look like one.

Chapter Ten
The Compostest with the Mostest

Superior to cheap garden supplies, are free garden supplies. Chapter 4 gave a long list of soil-building materials that could be had for absolutely no cost, as long as you're willing to compost it. Really, if the goal is to grow food as easily and cheaply as possible, composting is de rigueur:

- Save money on your garbage bill.

- Save money on your yard waste bill.

- Save money on fertilizer.

- Save money on top soil.

- Save time and effort from having to acquire and transport fertilizer and top soil to your garden.

- Save time not bagging up yard waste.

So, maybe you thumbed through some of the amazingly-thick books on the subject of composting and got intimidated by all that stuff about Carbon-Nitrogen ratios and pile temperature and yada yada yada, and you decided you'd rather do something less complicated, like drive over to the nursery boutique and fork over your credit card.

Sigh. Composting is so much easier than it looks. Even the Bible used the very simple principle of composting to illustrate a point for one of the prophets over 2,500 years ago. As the story goes, one day God called to Jeremiah and instructed him to get a brand new belt, put it on and not let it touch water. Jeremiah does as instructed and wears the belt around town for a while. No doubt he got a lot of notice for it; the prophets weren't known for being snappy dressers.

> A quick search on Amazon revealed sixteen books devoted to the subject of composting.

God then instructs Jeremiah take off his nice belt and bury it somewhere. More time passes, after which God has the man dig it out again, whereupon Jeremiah makes the observation that the belt is "ruined and completely useless."[29]

Yep. Take linen, which is made from flax stems; add water, dirt and time to it, and it will decompose. God was making the point that morally, we're subject to decay, too. No argument there, but I'll stick to the composting significance, which is….

Wet dead stuff rots.

Compost, by definition, is the combination of dead stuff, water and time. Period. If you make a heap somewhere with those ingredients, then leave it alone, you will get something to spread in the garden eventually.

So, why so many books, and what makes them so thick? Well, the composting process can be significantly sped up and improved with a few tweaks. Those tweaks and the science behind them are what are interesting enough to inspire whole tomes on the subject. If you want to learn something of the nature and mechanics of good

---

[29] Jeremiah 13 NIV

composting, read on.

Bacteria drive this process. If you put the ingredients together, you don't have to go out looking for the germs to start breaking it down; they're everywhere, up to a billion of them per gram of soil They even float in the air. The very thought is creepy enough to make me want to take a long hot shower and scour with a wire brush, but this proliferation of microorganisms is a good thing, honest.

Several types of bacteria are at work here, and some are better than others at making garden soil. If you're not too fussy about what goes into your pile, a class of mesophilic bacteria will be the heavy lifters. They'll get the job done, but they're not in any hurry. They warm the pile slightly, in the range of 32-104F, 0-40C.

If conditions are right, thermophilic bacteria will kick in. You'll know they're at work because, as you may have guessed from their classification, the pile gets steamy-hot. (104-170F, 40-65C) Keep these guys happy and you get finished compost in weeks, not months. Additionally, this cooks any weed seeds, most other germs and repels bugs and other that might have crept into the mix. In fact, the pile can get so hot that the microbes heating it can end up even killing themselves in the process. This is the bar we're all trying to reach and stay with for our piles.

Those of you with real winters will be gratified to know that composting even happens as low as 0F, -20C, thanks to psychrophilic bacteria. Just don't hold your breath for the finished product.

Air is important because of the bacteria that need it to convert the nitrogen in the compost pile to nitrate, NO_3. The "hot" bacteria that do this are aerobic. Anaerobic microorganisms will make compost, too, but they'll make it slimy and smell awful in the process. That's your nitrogen converting to ammonia, NH_4 and entering a gaseous state, which is leaking into the air where it won't do your crops any good. Some of the ammonia will adhere to carbon if it encounters any, so add in those dry leaves if your nose is wrinkling. By the way, plants need their nitrogen in either the nitrate or ammonia form. Anything else is inaccessible to them. Still, you'd really rather work with air, because the aerobic bacteria work faster and won't have the long-suffering neighbors complaining that your place smells like a bog. Some of the gases released in anaerobic composting are also flammable, in high enough concentrations, which honestly isn't too likely in a typical backyard pile. Still, if you singe the spoiled purse poodle dog next door…

The way you inject more air into the system is simply to toss the pile by the fork-full from one place to another. This is what is known as "turning." Try to turn the pile as often as you can; once a week isn't too much.

Anaerobic composting is also a concern for some because it releases methane, CH_4 and nitrous oxide, NO. Both of these are greenhouse gases that are even more effective in trapping heat than carbon dioxide, CO_2, the most notorious of the Greenhouse Gas Gang.

Water is integral to composting. What do mummies high up in the mountains in Peru, the Dead Sea scrolls well below sea level, and ancient Egyptian papyrus all have in common? That's right, they're really, really dry. Recall God admonishing Jeremiah not to get his linen belt wet while he was wearing it, but all bets were off once he buried it. Optimal compost moisture is always described in the books as "as wet as a wrung out sponge." Too much water drowns out the oxygen. Too little discourages the bacteria.

And here we go with the bacteria again. It always comes back to them, doesn't it? These need water to digest their food, just like we do. Thus, if you're going to err on this water thing, err on the side of too much. At least once a week, hose down your pile. Alternatively, you can arrange your watering system to lightly water the compost at the same time as your plants. On a drip system, this might look like a hose with a few emitters on top of the pile. Just make sure to move the hose out of the way before turning the compost.

Nitrogen is a volatile element. This means it's easily dislodged from anything it's connected to, chemically-speaking. That's why nitrogen makes up some eighty percent of air, but plants are still desperate for it in the ground. Matter high in nitrogen, like manure, will compost rapidly all by itself, but this is disadvantageous to the gardener because the nitrogen will largely disappear into the atmosphere, and not stick around on something that can go into the ground.

Carbon is just the ticket for binding the ammonia that otherwise would be lost to the air. The perfect compost pile has a carbon-to-nitrogen ratio of about 25:1 through about 30:1. Terrific, but I didn't see the ratio printed on the lawn clippings. Graduate students spend a ridiculous amount of time assaying different plants and determining their exact C:N ratios, but even if I printed tables and lists of these things, it isn't terribly useful to the home gardener because we have what we have and that's what's going to get composted.

A home composter needs to know two important categories of information to successfully manage a compost pile:

1. Basic categories of carbon and nitrogen-rich plants

2. How to interpret pile characteristics to know what it needs

So, for the first part, just remember that if it's brown, i.e. shriveled and dried up, it's high in carbon. And if it's green, it's high in nitrogen. It really is that simple. Fallen leaves, for instance, range from 50:1 to 100:1 for their carbon-to-nitrogen ratio, but all you have to know is that adding them in some amount will "slow down" your pile and give the nitrogen something with which to bind. On the other side, fresh food scraps and grass clippings are plenty high in nitrogen, so they'll "disappear" quickly.

Cardboard, newspaper, and wood chips are very low in nitrogen. Use them sparingly in the compost pile as they will take a while to decompose. This makes them all perfect for making walkways in your garden plots. They also block out the sun from that part of the ground, which discourages weeds.

Alfalfa and clover are very high in nitrogen, which is how you can grow them in a plot, then just turn them into the soil to get the fertilizer turbo-boost from these green manures.

Hair, manure, seaweed and feathers don't exactly follow the "rule" about high-nitrogen green stuff, but they're all a big boost for this element, too.

In the second category, observation of what's in the pile will plainly tell you whether you need to add more carbon or more nitrogen. I'm betting you already know what to do, so take the quiz and see.

C:N Compost Quiz

Scenario #1:

The pile smells like old urine. You stick your fork in it and pull out a Swamp Thing's dinner. What do you do?[30]

Scenario #2:

You've been turning your pile for three weeks straight and nothing seems to be happening. You put your hand over the center of the pile and can't feel any warmth.[31] How can you get this party started?

Scenario #3:

The pile smells sour. Do you have to put up with this to get good compost?[32]

Scenario #4:

It's cold outside, but you're perfectly toasty next to your compost pile, which is wreathed in steam this frosty morning. So, what's the plan?[33]

Pencils up. How did you do? We're not grading on a curve, so if you missed one, you failed.

All this time, I've only mentioned a compost pile, as if it's just an unsightly heap on the ground. Well, that's exactly what it can be, and certainly that's the cheapest, easiest-access form compost can take. The compost is best if it can hold its heat, so mound it high and keep

---

[30] Add some dried leaves, pine needles or even a bit of shredded newspaper if that's all you've got. You need carbon. You probably also need air, so it needs to be turned, too

[31] Ha! This is a trick question because there isn't enough information here. Three things are possible if the pile isn't heating up. They are:
- There isn't enough moisture.
- You need some nitrogen
- The pile is already fully composted.

[32] The pile's too wet. Add carbon. If you were paying attention, you'd notice that the cure for a smelly pile, regardless of what that smell is, is carbon.

[33] Nothing. All is well. Be sure to turn the pile in a few days' time to keep it cooking.

it together as much as possible. Most books recommend that the pile be at least a cubic yard in size.

Compost containers run the gamut from those modular black plastic units with the removable tiers to old palettes lashed together, to the hay bale sides I mentioned in Chapter Four, to simple chicken wire fencing. The materials aren't all that important; just make sure you can remove the siding or fencing easily so it doesn't interfere with your ability to turn the pile.

There's one final oft-mentioned subject about compost piles, which has to do with the general concept of surface area. Obviously, the more surface, the more area for the all-important bacteria to reside and break down old vegetable matter. Many books therefore recommend that you shred everything going into the compost pile into tiny pieces.

Well, I've priced yard waste shredders/chippers and unless you've got a rich uncle who loves to spoil you, I say don't bother.

- They're expensive.

- Shredding everything is extra work.

- Tinier pieces mean fewer air spaces in the pile.

- If you want to use compost that has bigger pieces embedded in it, just separate out the pieces with a screen or pull the really big pieces out by hand.

- A few extra chunks aren't going to hurt most of your plants.

- Just leave out the stuff that's going to take forever to compost, like tree branches. They can go to your yard waste.

- You can shred some things yourself with a machete or by running over them with your lawn mower. You can even bury most of a weed trimmer with leaves in a garbage can, and then turn it on.

- Water does an amazing job of softening even seemingly tough stems and letting the bacteria work on them.

And now, the ultimate question: How do you know when you can actually use compost in your garden? Finished compost has the following characteristics:

- It's the color of rich dark chocolate.

- You can't tell what it used to be.

- It isn't hot anymore.

- When it's damp, it holds together slightly when squeezed in your hand.

- It just plain looks like great dirt to grow something in.

I'm a very lazy composter, to be honest. I don't keep my piles separate most of the time, so new inputs are always being added. When I'm ready to work something into my plots, I simply take a chunk from the most-finished part of the pile and spread it an inch or two thick where I'll be planting. If there is still a smattering of recognizable pieces in it, I'm not terribly concerned. I have yet to "burn" any plantings with too much acid because my compost wasn't completely "matured."

> The term "damping off" refers to a toxicity from fungi and other nefarious microorganisms in soil that particularly adversely affect germinating seedlings.

I do cheat just a little bit, though. When I want to start seedlings indoors, I usually buy a bag or two of potting soil, and use my half-done compost to line the bottom inch of each pot, filling up the rest with the store-bought stuff. Garden books will tell you that you should microwave your home compost soil for 30 seconds to avoid damping off, but I've yet to encounter a problem, so I'm often lazy about that, too.

In any case, the cost of a couple of bags of potting soil each year is "cheaper" to me than the extra work involved in curing and tending my compost pile to perfection. Like I said, this book is all about keeping the effort and expense of gardening to a minimum. I'm not a hobbyist; I want cheap, healthy food with as little effort as possible. My apologies if this offends a few purists out there!

Other than that, my compost is my fertilizer, with very few other inputs. I haven't bought store-bought fertilizer in years, and yet the food keeps coming. Compost is truly the cheapest, easiest way to get what your vegetables need so you get what you need to eat.

Chapter Eleven
A Little Goes a Long Way

When I think of a lot of agricultural production in a very little space, naturally I'm reminded of the 1917 Bolshevik Revolution. I mean, who wouldn't be?

All right, let me explain. If you recall your Modern Russian history, the Reds overthrew the Czar, and swiftly went about turning Russia into the Communist ideal. This new utopian fantasy was based on the teachings of Karl Marx, which was equal parts social engineering and economic experiment, carried out on a massive scale.

Socially, Marxist teachings declared that men were really nothing more than the sum of their abilities and that the "class struggle" brought on by inequality of wealth was what resulted in all the ills of the world. Eliminate that imbalance and meet all basic needs, so the argument goes, and the "workers" will all be happy and productive, even to the point of altruism.

To bring about all this "equality," the Communists had to have an all-powerful central government to direct and control the means of virtually all production in the country. The farms were no exception to this nationalization of industry, consolidating after 1928 into large collectives with the intent of utilizing economies of scale to eliminate inefficiencies in crop cultivation.

Former independent farmers were now part of these large-acreage enterprises, expected to work the fields they no longer owned for the good of the whole Soviet Union, and for the same wage regardless of the amount of effort they put into it.

At the same time, the State did allow small private plots, intended just to vary the farm family's diet a bit. All told, they never measured more than four percent of the total arable acreage of the USSR.

So, care to venture a guess which land dropped precipitously in productivity, resulting in the starvation of millions, and which land produced almost a third of the Soviet Union's agricultural output through the black market?

The point is, if you're motivated, you really can grow an amazing amount of food in a very small space. Even apartment dwellers with nothing but a sunny balcony can grow their own salads and herbs in containers.

Never forget what plants need: sun, water, nutrients. I once saw a hydroponics operation where the "sun" was artificial light in the proper electromagnetic wavelength. The water and nutrients were misted on the bare roots as the plants dangled in midair, propelled through the building on a long conveyer belt. Honestly, it looked like a lot of work and electricity to me, but the plants looked satisfied, and well-traveled, so who am I to oppose the wave of the future?

There are some real advantages to growing in a small area. There's less digging, and inputs can be broadcast that much more easily. Movement is more efficient because there's less of it to get from place to place. Here are a few ways to maximize the minimum.

Grow in squares, not rows. Rows are for mechanization and inefficient watering practices, and they don't make the most of limited space. Make your planting areas as wide and long as you can while still being able to reach the innermost plants inside, then plant in a staggered pattern that gives them all a little "elbow room."

Reach for the sky. Prop up vines and bushy plants to grow in an upward direction. Tomato cages work for more than just tomatoes, and poles work for more than just pole beans. Heavy fruit can be supported on a trellis with old pantyhose.

Make a lot of small plantings. You want green beans, but you only need enough to eat, not to give away. So grow only 25 or so bean plants at a time. Three weeks after the first planting, start another one somewhere else, so that when the first planting is tapering off, you're getting some from the next. This beats taking up all the space to grow 50 plants at once, resulting in a scenario of feast followed by famine.

Start seedlings elsewhere. If you start seeds in the ground, gaps will be left where some failed to germinate. Seedlings also don't need a lot of room when they're small, so a single pot on a sunny windowsill may be all you need for a whole crop planting, while the ground it'll use is currently otherwise engaged with larger plants busily making food.

Out with the old, in with the new. As a corollary to the last tip, keep every part of your garden in constant productivity for as long as stuff will grow out there during the year.

Be a deep thinker. For water conservation purposes, you want to encourage your roots to dig down anyway. Make sure they've got enough good soil to do it. Roots that go down need less from the sides. A couple of feet at least would be great for this.

It may be tempting to skip making aisles between plantings, or making them very narrow, but I don't recommend this. More time and food will be wasted if it's difficult or impossible to maintain the plants and access the harvest.

That's pretty much it. Before you start grousing at me about how little useful information I'm including in this chapter, consider what Victory Gardens, California agriculture and Soviet peasant plots all have in common. That's right; they're all a lot of food from small spaces. So I've been covering how to economize land area all along.

Besides, "those who don't remember the past are condemned to repeat it."

Chapter Twelve
Time on Your Side

My thoughts get a little random when I'm bored. Take, for instance, the concept of time. This is the variable at fault for our failing so far to come up with the Grand Unification Theory. This Holy Grail of physicists will finally join quantum laws with general relativity. So, what's the problem? Time. The only way to balance out the equation is to cancel out time, but that would mean that time is a constant and we're all therefore living in the same instant of it for the whole of our lives. I get really depressed about this because usually when I think about it, I'm unloading the dishwasher.

Since letting my mind wander is clearly a hazard for me (and for every poor soul who hangs out with me), prudence dictates that I avoid the monotony that incites it wherever possible. Certainly some of the work in the garden is pretty dull. This chapter explores a few ways to get out of doing it.

Replace yourself with automation. Water timers cost about ten bucks, plus batteries. Adjust the length and frequency of watering on the little dial gizmo, then sit back and let the plants take care of themselves for a while. Bonus: You can go on a vacation without worrying that you'll come back home to a stand of dead sticks.

Weed early and selectively. When weeds are young, they're shallow. That means you can rip them out of the ground with a simple swipe of a hoe. Pre-flowering weeds can also go into your compost. If you wait until they've developed a strong taproot, you've at least tripled your workload. On the other hand, if the weeds aren't directly competing for nutrients, sunlight or water with what you're growing, and you're busy, let 'em lie. In that case, it's simply a matter of the aesthetics. If your food doesn't care, then you don't have to care, either.

Get your compost to turn itself. Okay, this one's a bit pricey, so it won't work for everyone, but there are some nifty compost containers out there in the general shape of a barrel that you can spin to tumble the contents. I'm intrigued by these because they're self-contained to better hold in moisture, their color absorbs heat and retains it well, and because the compost is turned so often, the finished product should be available much faster than by conventional means. I don't have one yet, but competition for these tumblers is heating up almost as fast as the compost in them. Prices are finally (slightly) sub-stratospheric, but I'm going to have to wish for one, or three, a bit longer. Run an Internet search on "compost tumbler" to see the range for yourself.

Use mulch. The definition of mulch is anything that covers the ground. You'll see everything from old carpet to plastic sheeting to wood chips called "mulch." In this case, I'm thinking primarily of a few inches of leaves. This leaf cover has come up before in the context of a winter covering for garden plots. The time savings here is in letting the soil build itself while you hibernate for the winter.

There is time savings using it later in the year, too. Mulch helps the soil to retain water while depriving weeds of sunlight, so you'll water and weed less.

Don't fuss over your compost. As long as the compost is kept moist, it'll rot, whether you turn it often, balance the C:N ratios just so, et cetera, et cetera. If you need to neglect something, neglect the compost, not the food. It's really easy to get compost to the "close enough for government work" stage that lets you toss it, chunks and all, into the plots where transplanted seedlings can work with it just fine. That potting-soil perfection involves a lot more effort to achieve, which may not be worth it when a couple of cubic feet of the stuff goes for five bucks at a discount warehouse.

A spot of tea makes for easy fertilizer. Trips to the Prissy Plant Pavilion for an official-looking "Probiotic, Laboratory Tested, Good

Housekeeping Seal of Approval"- type fertilizer take time and money, but you may feel compelled to do it if your plants don't seem to be all that they can be. Put the keys and credit cards down, and try brewing up some compost tea first.

This stuff couldn't be easier to make. Simply dump a shovelful of your most finished compost into a bucket of water. Let it steep for anywhere from a day to a week, then strain out the solids. The resulting black gold now has a high concentration of everything a plant could possibly want, in a form that the roots can uptake quickly. In fact, it may be too much of a good thing. Cut it two-to-one with water to see how the plants react first, to avoid "burning" them with such high-powered nitrogen.

Beware of the chlorine that might be in your city water supply, which can kill off all of the good fungus and other microorganisms that we're trying to encourage to multiply in the tea. Either use filtered water or fill your bucket at least a day before you start steeping, to allow the chlorine to outgas first.

About now, you may be asking yourself what minimum amount of time is needed to spend in the garden and still get a fair return with the food. Honestly, I think it averages out to about an hour a week, all told, with a couple of caveats. First, I'm assuming that you have automatic watering. Second, I'm not including the time to harvest; I count that as part of food preparation just as if you walked to your refrigerator or pantry and picked your choices off of the shelves. If you're okay with those quibbles, then one hour a week of pure work in the garden is what I think it takes to get a reasonable amount of food from it.

I do admit though, that the input of gardening effort isn't even throughout the year. In the summer and the winter, the average is less than an hour, but the spring and autumn are periods of new plantings and transition, so you'll be busier then.

Even from week to week, the "hour" may not be a constant. One week I may not do anything at all; the next, I might spend part of the morning turning compost, starting a few pots of seeds, tearing out some spent plants, working a shovelful of compost into a patch, and then transplanting something into the space. When I punch out, I find

I've put in two hours. Anyway, my point is that, when averaged over the year, I think it's reasonable to say that a person could get away with only fifty-two hours of gardening labor in order to grow, say, half of all the fruits and vegetables he consumes in that year.

I also say that this amount of work competes well with the time and effort involved in shopping for fresh produce at the supermarket. If the cost and taste are factored in, there's no competition at all!

Chapter Thirteen
Compatible Animals

"If we could talk to the animals,
learn their languages
Think of all the things we could discuss
If we could walk with the animals,
talk with the animals,
Grunt and squeak and squawk with the animals,
And they could squeak and squawk and speak and talk to us."[34]
   – Dr. Doolittle

O ne fine spring day before I knew better, I spent a king's
ransom on composted chicken manure. I know it's good for
the garden and all, but I have a hard time getting excited
about spending money on excrement for any reason. While I was
spreading it all around, still grumbling about the precious metals these
animals must've been eating to justify the cost of their droppings, I
got to musing about the relationship between plants and animals.

Animals feed plants, which feed animals, which feed plants,
which feed and on and on and on. A vegetable garden is one side of a
tight symbiosis, without the other side of which you're at a
disadvantage, because you'll have to supply it artificially. That can

---

[34] Music and lyrics by Leslie Bricusse

entail anything from making friends with someone who owns a horse, to buying bagfuls of poop and trying not to feel stupid when the credit card bill arrives.

But what if the supply isn't artificial? Are there animals out there that you could keep, that don't require a lot of time, space or maintenance and that could help the garden, too?

I should mention: I live in an affluent, very suburban neighborhood. Vegetable gardens are not the norm in this area. When I told a friend I was moving here, she rolled her eyes and remarked, "You're going to become one of the 'ladies who lunch.'"

Psshh, yeah, right. Several years later, it's obvious to many that I'm a bit eccentric. The neighbors don't mind, though, and do you know why? I make sure my compost doesn't smell and I've picked animals that are quietly compatible with growing food *and* an upscale location. Rest assured, "Jersey Cow" isn't on the list of "Animals Compatible with Urban and Suburban Vegetable Gardening." Here are a few that are, though.

Worms are speedy compost-makers. Let them munch and expel your kitchen scraps instead of going out to the heap; you'll have ready compost in a fraction of the time. Vermiculture has long been respected for its garden enhancements; in fact, without worms in your regular soil, your plants would be in a world of hurt. Earthworms, i.e. the kind in your garden, are hard to raise outside of your dirt, so some variety of red worms are your best bet. You can buy these from the Internet by the wriggling, writhing pound and set them up at your site right away. Supplies to keep worms happy could not be simpler:

1. A shallow box that drains liquid while keeping the worms inside.

2. Some kind of bedding, like shredded newspaper, cardboard, leaves. Make sure the bedding is wet.

3. A handful of dirt for the worms to have grit for digesting their food.

4. Kitchen scraps in the ratio of one pound per every two pounds of worms every day

Maintaining worms is a snap. They don't like to be too cold or too hot, so keep them from 50-80 degrees F (10-27C). Keep them a little moist. The food you'll give them will help with that. Just toss in what you would've put in compost anyway. And that's pretty much it. There's no need to walk them, groom them or give them toys.

Not long ago, a story appeared in our local paper about a guy who started raising red worms to feed his pet turtles. Well, the worms multiplied beyond what he needed, so he started selling some to others. One thing led to another, and, a year and a half later, he expects to clear six figures in worm sales for the year!

The other nice thing about worms is that they reproduce quite readily if their conditions are right. You can start with one pound of worms and let them grow to the ideal operation size for you and your food availability; after that, you can get your friends started on them, too.

I've raised worms before, but I quit after a few months. Chances are good that I was doing something wrong, but I had three problems with them:

1. The worms always had an off odor to them, and I never could figure out how to fix that. I've since read that I was feeding them too much.

2. Ants around my house were somehow very attracted to the worm bucket. It didn't look like the worms were much bothered by the insects swarming all over them, but I was pretty grossed out.

3. I couldn't figure out how to be able to leave for a few days without finding someone to take care of them. See the first problem for why I was loathe to call in that kind of favor.

Still, someone else wants to set me up with some worms, so I'm probably going to give it another shot. Worm castings (i.e. poop) don't burn plants with excessive acid like fresh or half-done compost can, so you can use it as soon as you can scoop it out of the box.

Honey Bees are surprisingly low-maintenance. They can find their own food, thank you, and when they do, your well-pollinated garden will flourish. Theirs is a well-organized, high-functioning society. They keep themselves warm through all but the coldest winters. Really, bees don't need your help to flourish at all. However, if you want honey, provide them with a nice easy-access box to make it in. And if you want them to be as healthy and productive as possible, give them medicine to combat the various parasites that are common to bee populations.

The day-to-day maintenance of honey bees is almost nil. The bulk of the labor comes with getting started on your apiary, collecting and processing the honey and dividing populations when your successful bee colony grows too big for your space. All told, the total time commitment is less than forty hours a year.

There are some drawbacks to keeping honey bees, however. Veteran beekeepers report that yes, you will get stung once in a while. Don't expect their sympathy, either. The pros will insist it was your fault, usually because you were clumsy and provoked the bees, or you picked a cold and windy day to bother them. They are also quick to point out that bees die when they

Some studies suggest that bee venom is actually therapeutic in treating a variety of ailments, most notably arthritis. "A sting a day keeps the doctor away?" Hmmm.

sting, so they are most reluctant to do so unless they think they are under attack. The old-timers will allow that after a while, you build up a tolerance to bee stings, so that your skin hardly reacts to the venom. Still, if you're allergic to bee venom, do not take up beekeeping!

There is also a fair amount of equipment involved, depending upon how easily you want to access your bees and honey. The bee box is fairly complicated, with specific size and spacing requirements between panels.[35] Run an Internet search on "beekeeping plans" or "apiary plans" and you'll find several designs

---

[35] "Bee space" is the crawl space clearance (.3 to .4 inches/.75-.9cm) that bees are most comfortable moving around in. If the space is too big, they'll close the gaps with wax, which makes it harder for beekeepers to pry out the honey panels.

for bee boxes that you can build yourself. This is a cheaper alternative to buying them, but you have to be handy.

You'll need some protective clothing, though not as much as you might think. (Most beekeepers work without gloves, believe it or not!) A full "moon suit" isn't really necessary; for the most part, if you wear long sleeves and enough layers too thick for stingers, bees can't bother you much. Be sure to use duct tape to close anywhere a bee could crawl in, like up your pants leg. A stiff, wide-brimmed hat with netting keeps them off of your head and neck, and lets you see what you're doing.

A smoker blows thick smoke at bees to subdue them, which is also nice to have for major operations on the hive, such as stealing some of their honey. (Bees can get a little snippy about that!) You can also buy spray cans of artificial "smoke," but they are not reusable like traditional smokers, and more expensive.

Honey extracting equipment is pricey, too, but I found a beekeeper's club in my county that will let you use their equipment if you pay the membership fee, which was much cheaper. The bonus is that you don't have to store all that stuff at home. I highly recommend that you find a club or talk to local beekeepers. They can point out local sources for obtaining the bees and equipment, and save you from making a lot of rookie mistakes. Books are good, too. I found *Beekeeping for Dummies*, by Howland Blackiston, to be especially good at telling it like it is for the neophyte.

Wild bees naturally inhabit your area, like Mason bees, Blueberry bees, and Hornfaced bees. (Honey bees can thrive in the wild, too, but I had to make some kind of distinction, so humor me.) Sure, you won't get honey from them, but they are still essential to pollinating the garden, so do what you can to encourage them.

Many wild bees thrive if they have a little hole in wood about 5/16th of an inch wide and several inches deep. It's easy to make a simple block of wood with dozens of these holes for them. Do make sure the wood isn't cedar or redwood, which repels bugs, including bees. Hang it up somewhere, and no more labor is required from you, but you've done your part to give native species a leg up. Many native bees will pollinate in colder weather than honey bees can, so you've extended your productive garden season, too.

Native bees will eventually make a mess in the holes, full of old molted exoskeletons, dead nymphs and parasites, so either clean out your old blocks or make new blocks for them every winter. Some people get really fancy, and line the holes they make with baking parchment or wax paper (which these bees like to chew) that can be removed each year. That looks somewhat labor-intensive to me, but if you're really a bee lover, it's an option. Just make sure to account for the thickness of the paper when drilling the holes.

Catfish can be raised in a barrel. Not only that, but they thrive on worms, so if you've already got a box of those going, you have little other expense. Make sure that the water you use for them is non-chlorinated, or they could die. And they need oxygen pumped into the barrel.

To read all about how one couple raised their catfish with this method, go to:

http://www.tabletophomestead.org/Raising%20Fish%20In%20A%20Barrel.html

You'll have to replace some of their water every day to keep the catfish from polluting themselves. Wastewater from the fish is also high in nitrogen and other nutrients, so it's terrific for your crops.

I can't speak with any authority on this subject because no one in my family likes catfish all that much. Still, I'm intrigued by the notion of forming a whole web of mutual benefit between worms and fish, fish and garden, garden and worms and back again.

Other fish can be raised for the table, as well as to help the garden. Aquaponics is the agricultural discipline that takes advantage of the natural symbiosis between fish and plants by raising both together, and it's been getting a lot more commercial attention lately.

One of my kids and I built an aquaponics set-up for a Science Fair project.[36] Encouraging the natural symbiosis that exists between fish, bacteria and plants is very simple:

- Fish live in a tank. You need to feed them fish food.

- Plants grow, usually from seed, in pea gravel, and you supply nothing else directly.
- A pump brings water from the tank up to another tank.

---

[36] The judges liked it, too. He won first place for his grade at his school.

- The holding tank releases water at intervals to the plants in the gravel. (The intervals are needed to provide oxygen to the roots, or they would drown. In our case, we used a toilet flapper that opened when enough water entered the tank to pull a weight down.)

- The water is cleaned by the plants and drained back into the fish tank. The splash also oxygenates the water for the fish.

What's really happening is all about the Nitrogen Cycle. The fish waste produces ammonia, which is toxic to them, and not easily usable by plants. However, two types of bacteria present in soil and air (there's that creepy, crawly unclean feeling again!) quickly go to work, converting the NH_4 to first NO_2, nitrite and then to NO_3, nitrate, which plants just happen to love. They then strip out the nitrates, which are harmful to the fish. So successful is the system that no other fertilizer is required for the plants!

It takes a few weeks for the bacteria to be present in enough quantities to fully convert all the ammonia to nitrates, but once the tank is properly "cycled," as it's called, it works beautifully. Our system grew very good lettuce, which we enjoyed in our salads, but I've seen crops from tomatoes to onions grown with similar success.

> If you want to see how to build your own small aquaponics set-up, I highly recommend:
>
> www.aces.edu/dept/fisheries/education/documents/barrel-ponics.pdf

The real advantage of aquaponics is that the fish can be edible, too. Large commercial systems usually use some type of Tilapia, which is a fish native to the tropics that tastes pretty close to trout. Tilapia are algae-feeders that can withstand salt and fresh water and live in confined places. They don't like to get too cold, but they can take pretty high heat. We tried to get Tilapia here in California, but after months of fruitless searching for a hatchery that would sell me some, I had to give up. For our experiment, we used goldfish and minnows.

One thing to consider with an aquaponics system is the cost of the electricity to run the pump. We set ours on an automatic timer to run only two hours a day because when I worked out the math, running it all day would have cost us more than just buying fish sticks at the grocery store.

You can also buy an automatic fish feeder so you can get away for a few days and let the system run on its own, though in my experience, the water level gets low after that much time, lost through splash and evaporation.

To quantify the work involved in running an aquaponics system, I'd say it was no more than two minutes a day, mostly to feed fish and check for leaks or whatnot. Raising fish for food might be a bit more work if you wanted to manage their breeding. Still, it's something to consider if you can find a fish you like to eat, that can also thrive in this environment.

> The Farollones Institute once sponsored the Integral Urban House. This was a typical house on a city lot, but modified to be as independent as possible, including a fish tank with a fly trap suspended overhead. The fish never needed feeding; they just ate what dropped from the trap.

Toads are very beneficial to gardens in that they eat pests that attack your plants. So long as your garden is pesticide-free, they'll be happy with a cool, moist shady haven like a small rock garden or a large terra cotta pot on its side, half-filled with dirt, to call home. (Make sure they have an escape route out the back to get away from predators.) Run an Internet search on "toad house" if you want to see the endless imagination of children through their decorating schemes.

Toads eat at night. If you have one of those solar-powered lights that comes on at night, put it near the toad habitat to attract insects and make it easy for your little buddy to get his fill. Other than that, toads are happiest if they're just left alone.

Rabbits can eat kitchen scraps to supplement their regular feed. Their manure is really high in the Big Three nutrients a garden needs. Rabbits are quiet and have the added advantage that they can breed, well, like rabbits.

Maintenance for these creatures would mostly entail keeping them in a comfortable temperature, cleaning up after them and feeding them. Initially, there's the work and/or expense of providing a suitable hutch for them, too. Do consider that if you want leave town for a few days, you'll need someone to look in on them.

Keeping worms is a simple matter if you have rabbits; just keep their box below the hutch so they can feed on the manure. Some commercial rabbit breeders thus create three viable products to sell (rabbits, worms and castings) with the effort it takes to produce one.

If you are going to breed rabbits, as opposed to just having a fluffy pet or two, you also have to figure out what you want to do with them. The more squeamish among us can try to make a go of selling them as pets for extra cash, but that side business comes with its attendant extra time requirement.

Rabbit meat is supposed to be delicious. I haven't tried it myself, but if you raise them for food, you can maybe do something interesting with the pelts, too. Again, factor in how much time it will take versus the time you have.

Chickens are so easy, and provide so much for the home garden, I don't know why everyone's not keeping them. Roosters are ornery and too noisy for most neighborhoods; city ordinances often outlaw them. But hens are reasonably quiet, produce about a cubic foot of manure every year,[37] and in their first two years can lay over 200 eggs a year each, tapering off a bit every year thereafter. That's right, no rooster is required to get unfertilized eggs.

Chicken manure is fantastic for the home garden. It has more nitrogen, phosphorus and potassium than the manure of horses and cows. Only rabbits have better garden poop than chickens do. It's got whatever micronutrients the chicken's been eating, too. It'll burn plants if dumped on the ground fresh, but add it to the compost and watch it heat up the pile. Chickens are worth keeping for their poop alone.

But that's not all! The eggs are nothing to sneeze at. We saw eggs double in price in less than a year this last year. Fortunately, chicken feed didn't experience as high a jump, so now we're getting our eggs for much cheaper than we can buy them even by the five dozen at our local warehouse store. Before the huge spike in prices, we were running about even. The average chicken in her prime lays about an egg every 25 hours or so. (Unless you keep their coop well-

---

[37] No, I didn't measure this; I got the information off of the Internet. It fits with what I observe, however.

lit for at least sixteen hours a day, they'll molt[38] and skip egg production for the winter.)

Run an Internet search on "Super Foods," and you'll get dozens of lists of highly nutritious fare. Notice that eggs are almost always in the top ten of any of those lists. Eggs have really good-quality protein and every major vitamin in them except for C. (Kale shows up on these lists a lot, too, but unlike kale, eggs can be prepared in a large number of different ways and taste good.)

> The Egg Board is only too happy to provide extensive nutrition information about eggs on its website, if you're curious.
>
> http://www.incredibleegg.org/health nutrients.html

Since one key point of having a vegetable garden is to provide highly-nutritious, good-quality food to your table, raising chickens is perfectly compatible with that goal.

Call me a wimp, but I also like that I don't have to kill anything to obtain such an amazing source of complete protein. I can also give myself a big pat on the back that my eggs come from humanely-raised[39] animals.

Now what would you expect to pay? But wait, there's more. For those of you made of sterner stuff than I, you can have chickens for their meat, too. If they're laying hens past their producing prime, bear in mind that they'll be tough, so you'll have to stew them in your slow cooker for the day to tenderize them. Cockerels (boy chicks) cost much less than pullets (girl chicks) at feed stores. They reach a good eating weight in about six to eight weeks. Unfortunately, they start crowing in about four weeks, so consider how you're going to handle the noise while you're raising them.

The whole feather-plucking thing looks tedious to me, but apparently if you first plunge the carcasses in really hot water for thirty seconds, it's much easier. Remember that feathers are terrific for compost. Chicken meat is also a very healthy food, so these birds are two sources of high-quality food in one. (In my case, the therapy

---

[38] Molting involves losing their old feathers and growing new ones in rapid succession. The poor chickens sure look awful when they're going through it.

[39] That is, now that I've finally gotten the kids to stop sending the chickens down the slide on their play structure.

bills for the kids would far outweigh any economic benefit from stewing a beloved pet!)

Basic chicken maintenance is practically effortless. They drink twice as much as they eat, so access to water is critical. We bought an automatic waterer that's connected to a garden hose, so all I have to do is clean out the box where the water comes in once in a while. We have to replenish the feed once every four days or so. Real farming books tell you to clean out the coop at least once a year(!); I prefer more like once a week for basic one-minute surface scraping, and once a month for shoveling the bottom layer into the compost. Other than that, I'm pretty much just out there to say hello and collect eggs.

Before I got chickens, I asked a friend how much time she put into hers. Her answer was ten minutes a day. Months later, when mine were established, I came back, wanting to know what she did with the other nine minutes. She couldn't think of anything either. They really are that simple. I can get away for a few days and they can take care of themselves, too. I usually just get a neighbor to pick up the eggs. No one ever seems to mind that chore.

Chicken feed is reasonably cheap, though like all grain-based foods, it's been rising lately at a good clip. The good news is that you don't have to rely completely on chicken feed. Noxious weeds from my garden, the ones that flower before I can get to them, go through bird gizzards before they go to the compost. Really, most weeds and spent vegetable plants can go to them for "pre-composting" first.[40] They get so excited when you give them bugs and caterpillars and …. (drum roll) … worms! These are a perfect source of protein for them.

If you have leftover bread that hasn't molded yet, I've read it's not great for compost because it "slows it down." No problem. The girls'll take care of that for you. They gladly accept kitchen scraps, too. Crush their own eggshells and give it to them; they recycle the calcium into new eggs for you. My sister-in-law used to feed hers anything from leftover hamburgers to pasta. She calls them "pigs with wings." If you let them roam, up to forty percent of their intake will be grass, and you'll have noticeably fewer bugs around. Don't allow them directly in the garden, though. They like young tender

---

[40] Potato and tomato leaves are toxic to humans, so I don't give them to my girls, but I've caught them nibbling on them without any obvious distress.

plants, too.

Chickens provide a certain amount of entertainment value. If they see you, they'll come a-running in the hopes that you've got something interesting for them to eat. They have a certain sense of play, too, which is fun to watch. If you can get one to catch a Frisbee, I want to see the video!

The largest amount of time and expense you'll need for chickens is the initial set up and establishment of your flock. Feed stores have chicks usually in the spring, though some keep them in stock all year round. They're usually three bucks or less to buy, and the rule of thumb is to get the same number of chickens that you have members of your family. However, be sure to check your local ordinances; some of them limit the number of hens you can have before they're considered livestock instead of "pets." Over that magic number, and the ordinances will prescribe certain distance requirements where the animals must be kept from neighbors' homes.

Early on, chicks are vulnerable to cold and illness, so you have to protect them and keep them warm. This looks a lot like a cardboard box with a heat lamp. They foul their food and water often, so at least twice a day you're having to muck that out a bit. None too bright, these birds.

Once the gals are ready to brave the outside world, a coop is really nothing more than an enclosed space with a box or two for laying eggs in. Coops come in an amazing variety of sizes and shapes, but a few guidelines are helpful.

Here's a nifty website, all about how to raise chickens:

http://www.backyardchickens.com/

- Make sure the coop is an effective barrier from raccoons, rodents and other pests.

- Give them a bar to roost on; that's how they like to sleep.

- Make it a structure easy to clean. They are none too picky about where they poop.

- One laying box per every five chickens is fine.

- Make it easy for you to replenish food and access the eggs, since that's chiefly what you'll be doing for your birds.

- Commercial egg farms only give chickens about two square feet of space each. Make sure you at least double that to really let them stretch.

Chickens live upwards of eight years, but four is more the norm. Along the way, you won't have any veterinary bills. I've lost two chickens in four years, and in my experience, they seem fine right up until they keel over and die.[41] But they are amazingly hardy; withstanding even below-freezing temperatures if they can huddle together away from the wind for warmth.

Whew! This is a lot about chickens, but I wanted to give you a sense of the involvement required to successfully raise them. There's more though; get a good book on the subject or do some clicking around the Internet for more information before you take the plunge. Chickens are really a no-brainer for a gardener. If you want both sides of that symbiotic relationship between garden and animal, seriously consider starting your own little flock. You won't be disappointed.

Ducks and Geese have many of the same maintenance requirements as chickens, and are about as prolific egg-wise. Their eggs are a bit more nutritious, albeit with much more cholesterol, and store better than chicken eggs, too. Their manure isn't as high in nitrogen, but is higher in phosphorus. The deal-breaker for me is that they need a lot of water for drinking and swimming.

Turkeys eat more than chickens and take up more room, but have the same basic care requirements as smaller poultry. Books will tell you that turkeys and chickens have to be kept separate from one another, but I knew a family who raised them together, with seemingly no ill effects. The main reason to raise turkeys is for bragging rights at the Thanksgiving table, but the prices at local

---

[41] I think one of them ate a plastic yogurt cup that a kid left in their coop, and the other succumbed after several days of really hot weather. I should have put ice cubes in their water to help them cope.

grocery stores that time a year for frozen birds is so cheap, there isn't a good economic argument for them, I'm afraid.

Looking at all the tall grass I'm constantly mowing, I also looked into how hard it might be for a lazy gardener to have a goat or a sheep. I was thinking it might also be fun to have something that provides some kind of milk so I could make my own cheeses or something.

Ha. No way. Here's why:

- You can't have just one goat or sheep. They need companion animals.

- They'll eat grass if they have to, but they prefer all that yummy stuff in your garden.

- They can bust through all but the strongest fences… and can figure out a latch, too.

- Milking them is an every day, twice a day thing, and they need to be refreshed, that is, have new babies, every other year or so.

That's all my neighbors need, to find my goat in their pool one day. This looks like too much work for me. But I just had to check.

The 10 Stupidest Reasons to Raise Sheep, courtesy of FishWhistle Farms:

http://www.fishwhistle.com/dont.html

"Swine not?" you ask. Well, on the plus side, pigs don't have huge space requirements; only about twelve feet/four meters square. They eat just about anything, and grow from birth to upwards of 250 pounds (110+ kilograms) in as little as six months. You could probably make some money buying a piglet in the spring to sell at a livestock auction in the fall.

All the same, pigs are not compatible with gardens. The biggest reason is that their manure, like that of dogs, cats and people is too dangerous to use, due to the potential of disease-causing bacteria that can live in it. Also, being fairly intelligent creatures they, like goats, will get into mischief when bored, so they are more work than most of us want to take on.

Plants need animals and animals need plants. Even a householder with little time and available space has choices of low-maintenance animals that can greatly enhance the family's garden. Some of these animals can also improve the family's diet. All of them will save you money! If you can manage the responsibility, consider adding them to your home-grown grocery production line.

Chapter Fourteen
Food, Glorious Food!

My gardening years get names based on their respective bumper crops. 2007 was the Year of the Tomato. 2006 was the Year of the Pumpkin. I'm still eating pickles from the Year of the Cucumber before then[42]. This year is shaping up to be the Year of the Jalapeño, which is a bummer since I'm the only one in my family who'll even go near them.

That's just the nature of gardening. You can plan to the best of your ability, but you'll just never know perfectly what climactic and soil conditions for that year are going to favor what crops. So, besides eating until your family can't even look at another member of this year's bumper crop, or alienating all your friends with double armloads on their front porches, what could you do with all this food?

Let's back up to when the crop is ripe, but not yet overproducing, when you've got some vegetables ready for picking, but not enough to justify a whole meal out of them. This is the point where good meal planning makes all the difference. Often, part of the reason why you're suddenly dealing with excess is because you left the first gleanings on the plant, and when more caught up, suddenly you've

---

[42] That was also the Year of the Snow Pea, when the kids almost rioted after three straight weeks of stir fries and salads, all with, you guessed it.

got an overage.

Plan your meals to use even small amounts of garden produce if you can. It's too easy to let some go to waste because you didn't think it was enough to bother, but you went to all that work to grow it, so use it. You can make a lot of stews and stir fries with the dregs of onions, green beans, cabbage, celery, chard, etc.; just a little of each. Have friends over the dinner and they'll think you're quite the gourmet with so much variety in the meal. No need to make them any the wiser.

In the event that your daily meals don't take care of your surplus, consider longer-term storage. A good canning and preserving book would be very helpful for the following options.

Freezing preserves some foods for months, with relative levels of damage to the vegetable upon thawing. Just about anything can be frozen, it's just a question of how much will be lost in texture. Green beans and corn hold up reasonably well; tomatoes and potatoes turn to mush and rubber, respectively.

Blanching, which is dunking the vegetable in boiling water for 30 seconds or so before freezing it, kills enzymes that would degrade the vegetable further even in the freezer. Any good canning and preserving book will detail exactly what vegetables can be frozen and how to do it the best way possible.

My first book in the Simpleton Solution series, *Strategic Eating, An Econovore's Essential Guide,* details over a dozen different meal-planning options for using up bits and pieces of food from previous meals and the garden. If you're motivated to shave your food bill along with growing healthy food, this is a good resource.

Drying takes away the water that bacteria need to decompose the food. Peppers, most fruits and some varieties of tomatoes dry reasonably well. Again, canning and preserving books provide lots of detail on exactly how to dry specific fruits and vegetables. Sometimes, what's in the books doesn't fit with personal taste, though. For instance, I'd read that cucumbers dry well, but I thought they tasted terrible when I tried it during those desperate months of the Year of the Cucumber.

Cool storage is basically like the cellars of old, before refrigeration, and which some people still use today. Using a cellar can be tricky. Some vegetables need to be stored in high humidity, and some in very dry conditions. Some vegetables emit ethylene gas that can rot other vegetables. For instance, potatoes and onions do not store well together. Likewise, apples will brown bananas in no time. Many root crops can stay alive and crisp by "growing" in buckets of moist sand. If you've got a place that keeps a reasonably even 50-60 degrees F (10-16C) year round, you'll be able to store some crops, like pumpkins, for months. Consult a food preservation book to learn more.

Canning preserves food by sterilizing it with heat and then vacuum-sealing it so no new microorganisms can get to it. Some contents will discolor over time, but so long as the seal holds, food can last indefinitely.

I emphasized the importance of trying to eat as much food fresh as possible because that's when the nutrition is at its peak. Storing it by any means and for any length of time means that the food will lose some nutrition via heat, light or just plain time. Generally, drying and canning are worse than freezing, but usually freezer space is at a premium, so the other options have to be considered.

Storage is another way of extending your harvest. It's fun to eat your own blackberry jam and remember fondly the June harvest, in January. The more you can eat of your garden, the better your return on the investment of your time and effort.

Part IV
Pest Less, Stress Less

Chemical-free gardening is really the way to go when you're growing your own food.

- The kids can eat stuff right off the plant.

- Pesticides are expensive.

- Pesticides don't differentiate; beneficial bugs die right alongside the bad ones.

- Remember the planet? Hello?

You're not the only one who wants your food, however. I read an article in the newspaper once that instructed gardeners to just plan to "give" a tenth of their garden to the natural loss from various pests and not to worry about it otherwise. I laughed when I read that. What was that author smoking? Pests won't equitably divvy up the spoils with you. They aren't going to share. If the largesse is there and you don't do something to hide it, they'll take advantage of the bounty to breed like crazy until you have nothing. (I am still talking about garden pests; any resemblance to government programs is purely coincidental.)

But if you can't just poison or burn them, how do you prevail against pests determined to eat every last leaf? Turns out, there are ways, and ultimately, an organic garden is much healthier than a conventional one. As organic farming has gained more of a foothold in this country, researchers have been amazed at the yields of healthy, balanced cultivation.

Chapter Fifteen
Tires, Mattresses, Crops

What do all the items in the title of this chapter have in common?

Not sure?

I'll add a clue: Schedules.

C'mon…

One last puzzle piece: Shoulders.

Think about it…

Give up? These would all be Jeopardy answers in the category Things that Rotate.

Gardeners should not be growing the same crops in the same spaces year after year for several good reasons:

- Pests that specifically thrive on that type of plant will accumulate in that patch of soil.

- The soil will be depleted more rapidly in the specific nutrients that the one type of plant feeds on the most.

- Other nutrients that the crop doesn't use as much will build up to high, possibly toxic, levels.

- Other gardeners will think you're uncool and shun you.

Fine, scratch the last bullet point. But they sure won't thank you for cultivating enough cucumber beetles to share with them.

Good note-taking is very helpful in determining where to put your crops next year. Even if you can remember exactly where everything was last year, the best crop rotations need to account for placements over more years than that. Four is the minimum.

There are other considerations too. Some pests can target multiple related crops. For instance, if something was eating your tomatoes, you're not doing yourself any favors by planting potatoes in the same spot next year. That's because tomatoes and potatoes are close enough botanically that most pests for one can gorge on the other just fine.

Depending on the feeding needs of some crops, other crops that come behind them in that space can be either disadvantaged or encouraged by what the former tenant left for them. As an example, carrots in a high-nitrogen environment will grow hundreds of little feeder roots off of their main tap root, until they look hairy, which isn't very appetizing. Corn is a heavy nitrogen feeder, so you could plant your carrots after the maize has licked up most of the nitrates in the soil.

Crop rotation may seem like an unnecessary complication to gardening, especially for the small spaces we're growing in, but knowing something about how this works really is useful. With a little knowledge and planning, you won't spend any more time actually planting anything, and you'll ultimately save much time and effort by avoiding serious pest and soil issues down the line.

I have no interest in trying to make an actual living as an organic farmer, but the way Eliot Coleman writes about it, it looks almost easy. Coleman is the author of *The New Organic Grower*, which is an incredibly rich source of his extensive knowledge and research on all things organic in cultivation. This guy spends more time in university libraries looking up the most-recent studies on crop yields than he spends actually working amongst his five acres, but the vegetables are all the better for it. Anyway, on the subject at hand, he has this to say:

> **From his experience as a researcher at Rutgers, Firmin Bear stated that well-thought-out crop rotation is worth 75 percent of everything else that**

might be done, including fertilization, tillage, and pest control. In fact, I think this is a conservative estimate... To my mind, crop rotation is the single most important practice in a multiple-cropping program.[43]

So, there you have it. Keep reading!

Good crop rotation needs to keep several factors in mind:

- Crops close in rotation should not be related botanically.

- Crops close in rotation should ideally want different nutrients from the soil.

- Crops close in rotation should not share the same pests.

- Crops that cover the ground well can discourage weeds for successive crops.

- Legumes add nitrogen to soil, so they're good to grow before heavy feeders.

- Onions and many strong-flavored herbs like dill naturally repel many kinds of pests, so planting them in small groups among other crops can be beneficial overall.

- Remember how tall these crops are, and if they're going to block sun from others if they're transferred into the wrong space.

I don't exactly know what you intend to grow, so I can't give you specific crop rotation schedules, but this chapter should be enough to get you at least thinking about how you want to approach the challenge, not that it's really all that difficult. The simplest crop rotation would be simply to try not to grow the same thing in the

---

[43]Coleman, Eliot, *The New Organic Grower* ©1995 by Molly Cook Field, Chelsea Green Publishing, White River Junction, VT

same place for four years running. That'll likely provide a good eighty percent of the possible benefit from crop rotation.

So, what crops are botanically related to other crops? There are a few commonly-grown categories:

Brassicas are all part of the mustard family. They include turnips, radishes, kohlrabi, cabbage, Brussels sprouts, cauliflower, broccoli, mustard(!) and rape.[44]

Carrot family members include carrots, parsley, celery, fennel, dill, anise, caraway, chervil and coriander.

Cucurbits are populated by melons, cucumbers, squashes and gourds.

Goosefoot family members include beets, Swiss chard, quinoa, spinach and purslane.

Legumes include soybeans, green beans, lentils, peas and chickpeas.

Lilies comprise onions, garlic, asparagus, chives and scallions.

Nightshade family members include tobacco, tomatoes, tomatillos, potatoes, peppers and eggplants.

You can't go wrong if you simply avoid members of the same family when picking the next crop to go in any particular space.

Appendix A also details what I know about the botanical relationships and nutrient needs of specific crops, so consult that to further guide you. If you desire still more inspiration, I just ran an Internet search on "crop rotation" and got 932,000 hits, so resources abound!

---

[44] Rape is the plant from which we get canola oil. "Canola" is a made-up word to give "rape seed oil" a better footing the marketplace. Go figure.

Chapter Sixteen
Dealing with Common Pests

I sometimes don't know whether I should spend my time writing books for a living or conducting scientific experiments to find an important industrial use for slugs. All I need is one good application, and I'll be rich beyond my wildest dreams of avarice.

Yep, I have enough slugs to inspire the most mournful of country western songs. But here's the good news: they aren't really a problem in the garden anymore.

It turns out that **snails** and **slugs** go absolutely stupid for beer. Dig a shallow hole in the ground near the plants that are getting eaten, place a small cup with at least an inch of beer in it, and the little slime balls all make a bum rush for it. Just toss all the drowned snails and slugs into your compost when the container's full. (I'm sure if I put my mind to it, I could come up with a good joke here about attracting other slimy characters with malt beverages to clear out some of those losers from the dating scene, but that has nothing to do with vegetable gardening, and I'm way too classy for that kind of a cheap shot. That's my commitment to quality, for you, the consumer.)

This "beer it and forget it" method sure beats what one gardening book recommended, which was to go out at night with a flashlight and pick them off of the plants, one by one. I just don't have that kind of time, and I pity those who do.

And then there was the Great Disappearing Tomato Mystery from a few years back. We'd had a really wet, cool year so far, so my poor shivering, waterlogged tomato plants were barely doing much more than hanging in there, even as July approached. The cherry tomatoes were ripening first, one at a time, which made them all the more precious. I checked one, deemed it worthy of harvest for the next day, and went back inside. The next morning I popped out to retrieve it, and it was gone!

Well, there was another tomato almost ready, so I stopped dwelling on the first one. Come collection time, that one was also gone without a trace.

This happened over and over again. These weren't tomatoes with some tell-tale bite out of them, or dropped on the ground; they just vanished as soon as they were ripe. I began to question my sanity.

My tomato-loving husband finally put it together, and then he went to war against the thieves. He set the classic spring-loaded, skull-crushing rat traps with some peanut butter and placed them at the base of several of the tomato plants. Snap! Snap! Snap! In short order, we caught fourteen **rats** and **mice**.

In true hypocritical fashion, when we only slightly-injured one, the kids named him "Squeaky," and promptly pronounced their undying love for him, so we had to take him to a nearby open space area and let him go. We can set deadly traps, but we can't bring ourselves to look at those soulful little beady eyes to do the deed. If you're more humane, there are live traps you can buy to catch and release your rodent problem.

Onions and garlic are repulsive to most furry little creatures and bugs. Plant a few of these in and amongst some of your more vulnerable crops and you'll probably find that pests will move on.

If you rotate crops, you can probably outrun most bug and fungus problems, but other pests will want to enjoy the feast you're making out there. Here are a few ideas for dealing with some of the more common problems.

Aphids love so many types of plants, it's hard to get away from them completely, even with crop rotation. If you're not sure what they look like, they're little round pencil-tip-sized bugs of assorted colors that group up around stems and under the leaves of your plants, usually accompanied by lots of ants. These ants actually "milk" them for a stick-sweet substance that they produce.

I've read that the root cause as to why certain plants are

vulnerable to infestation is either not enough, or too much, nitrogen. In other words, no one really seems to know how to completely avoid them. When your plants are infested, you'll notice that the leaves curl, and the whole plant just generally weakens and produces very little. They attack roses, chard, green beans, artichokes, and more.

Organic gardening books will tell you to do one of two things: Spray them off with a hose, or mist them with a nice organic insecticidal soap. The first doesn't work because any water jet strong enough to knock them off usually shreds the plant first. Also, because the leaves often curl over them, they are largely protected from the onslaught. When I tried the second, they laughed at me, waggling their little round behinds at the spray bottle in mocking fashion. The pores on the plants got all nice and clogged with oils in the soap, so they suffered all the more.

I'm going to recommend the one thing that seems to have worked for me. Get a baby wipe or a wet tissue, and wipe them off where they've concentrated, that is, along the stems and under leaves. Repeat once a week or so when they've had a chance to regroup. You won't get them all, but you'll get enough of them that they can't do real damage.

Deer make even the most animal-loving gardener crazy. Before their first vegetable season, new residents to a deer-infested area get all dewy-eyed when they encounter the sleek beauty of these nimble-footed creatures. By the fall, they're swapping their favorite venison recipes.

You've no doubt tried all the smelly solutions, from cloves to human hair, which are supposed to send them off to eat your neighbors flowers instead, but none of them work for very long, so you have to apply the remedies over and over. The deer just wait until you exhaust yourself, then they chew your plants to the ground as soon as you turn your back.

The only foolproof remedy I've seen is a tall, sturdy fence. Eight feet isn't too tall; these animals can (almost) leap tall buildings in a single bound if they see your strawberries. Constructing the barrier will set you back a few hundred dollars, and it's a weekend project for a couple of people, but once it's done, you have a fighting chance against the deer. While you're at it, run three feet of wire mesh along the ground along at the base of the fencing to keep out **rabbits,**

groundhogs and **gophers,** too.

Squirrels don't generally bother with my garden, except in the autumn when they're collecting nuts. For some reason, anything round suddenly gets their attention then.

The damage they cause is almost comical. Your beautiful melons and squashes will look ripe and ready, but when you pick them, you'll find they've been completely hollowed out from the other side.

For some reason, I have more scruples about killing squirrels than I do roof rats and mice. They seem to more naturally belong where I live, and they're really cute when they chase each other around the big walnut tree out back. So, for me, a spring-loaded trap is out of the question.

A friend recommended that I wrap my ripening orbs in aluminum foil, of all things. It's a testament to my desperation that I tried it, in spite of the fact that I thought it was as silly an idea as putting the foil on my own head to keep out mind-control waves from outer space aliens.

Well, it works. Somehow the critters can't figure out that they can just shred the foil with their little paws any time they like. Shhh! Don't tell them!

Fusarium and Verticillium are two types of fungi that can adversely affect tomatoes, potatoes and peppers. The upper leaves of these plants wilt during the day and recover somewhat at night, but eventually the whole thing wilts, often right when the plant is starting to bear heavily, as the fungus plugs the water-bearing parts of the stems.

If you're buying seeds, you can specifically get varieties that are resistant to both types of fungus. On the back of the package, look for F and Vt. The other strategy is to give the fungus nothing good to eat for a while so concentrations die down. You may need to avoid planting tomatoes, peppers and potatoes for upwards of six years before it's safe to try again.

The Enigma: Suppose your plants are miserable, but you've looked at all the obvious possibilities and still have no idea what the problem is. What do you do?

- Try fertilizing with compost tea. Some minor pest problems will go away if the plant is healthy enough to fight them off.

- Take very careful note of all the symptoms. What leaves are yellow and how high up the plants are they? Is there any distinctive curling? Holes? Spots? Slime trails? Look at the dirt around the plant. Anything interesting? A few pictures of the patients wouldn't be amiss.

- Look for suspect bugs. Search under the leaves and along the stem and base of the plant for anything suspicious. You may have to do your sleuthing at night, too. Be able to describe anything you find very clearly. Again, get a picture so you can make your own "perp walk" of the suspects.

- Bring part of the plant to the local Prissy Plant Pavilion for inspection and recommendations. They have big fat books with pictures to help with diagnostics. Before they can sell you the expensive, non-organic remedy, however, run for your life.

- Troll the World Wide Web. What an incredible resource this is! You can search for various plant symptoms and see images of possible problems. Then you can find some answers on how to deal with them.

- Get another brain. More experienced gardeners abound in your neighborhood, in the county Master Gardener program (type "master gardener" in a search engine), on Web forums (type "gardening forums" in a search engine). Somebody will know something.

Organic gardening promotes a natural balance between pests and the beneficial creatures that eat them. This prevents any one bug from dominating the environment around your crops. Usually, a pest problem is a symptom of something out of whack. Look to the fecundity of your soil and the frequency of your water for clues. I'd like to tell you that the problem will be "not enough" for both, but sometimes the problem is overabundance. The specific plant has vulnerabilities as well, not all of which are known. Graduate students are still working away on yet more answers to some of these issues.

If all else fails, try planting your crop in another section of the garden. There's no reason to deprive yourself of that particular food while you try to "save" the first crop.

Conclusion
Money vs. Wealth

I magine being adopted by Bill Gates or Warren Buffet and suddenly being so filthy, stinking rich you could compost with shredded thousand-dollar bills.

Naturally, you order something positively exquisite to eat: Caviar from Russia, foie gras from France, and vegetables picked straight from the fields around the globe and flown in special hermetically-sealed, temperature-controlled compartments aboard their own private jets, in order to arrive to you only hours after they were growing.

Or you could just be you and roast a chicken for about five dollars, served with your own vegetables picked from the backyard right before dinner.

Who has the freshest, most healthful meal? Who therefore has the higher standard of living?

Prince Charles, of all people, really seems to get the distinction between money and wealth. The funds certainly aren't a problem for him. Doesn't he basically own Great Britain, with a healthy stake in Canada, Australia, the Virgin Islands and several other places? And he's got more polo ponies than the rest of us have socks.

However, His Royal Highness co-wrote a very enthusiastic, full-color (or should I say "full-colour") coffee table-type book all about organic gardening. My favorite picture is one of him crouching on the ground next to a pile of grubby-looking little potatoes, which the staff makes sure to grow because he has a particular fondness for them.

The Prince goes on and on about his compost, and how he's mandated classes for all the gardening staff to learn how to weave plant supports from sticks cut elsewhere on the grounds, and what kind of easy, low-maintenance ground covers adorn the many pathways between the different themed sections around one of his castles. He's so pleased to find innovative ways to do more with less, and to increase food yields on his property and so on. Clearly, he revels in the true wealth that comes from his soil.

The Prince of Wales doesn't touch much on specifics, so I didn't learn anything new per se, but it was an entertaining read nonetheless, because as I flipped through the glossy pages it kept crawling through the back of my mind: If there's anyone who doesn't have to worry about where his meals are coming from, it's him! And yet, his money isn't what makes him feel so sated.

There's money. Then there's wealth. Money can be part of a means to a better lifestyle, but wealth is that lifestyle. Money is limited. Beyond a certain threshold, money rapidly loses its ability to add real value to your life. Will a multi-million dollar mansion keep the rain off of me any better than my own home? Will designer clothing protect me any more than my Chez Target off-the-clearance-rack duds, or really look better? Is the warm water at an expensive spa any more comfortable than the same temperature in my own bathtub? Here's the most important question: Can I buy true friends or a loving family?[45]

Wealth is comfort and peace and safety. Wealth is health. Wealth is having a skill-set that maintains and enhances your survival. Others in the world would give every penny they had for things we can still take for granted.

Growing your own food certainly isn't all there is to achieving wealth, but it does teach important skills and gives you the freshest, most nutritious meals possible beyond what mere money can buy. Any discernable increase in the quality of your life is an increase in true wealth. In that sense, looking out at a garden full of food is like

---

[45] I read that some elderly people in Japan actually rent actors to pretend to be their loving children and grandchildren for a set period of time. Isn't that just the saddest thing you ever heard?

perusing a healthy bank statement.

The heckler in the back asks a good question: If growing food is so wealth-enhancing, how come most family farmers are dirt-poor? Well, that's for a lot of reasons.

- They're not really poor in one sense because they're healthier than most and they'll never starve.

- Carla Emery, who wrote *The Country Living Encyclopedia*, put it best, and I'll paraphrase: "Farming is the only business where you buy retail and sell wholesale."

- As a corollary to that last point: If you're just growing food for yourself, you can do that in just a portion of your spare time, little space and no fancy equipment. But if you're doing this for a living, much more time and expense is required, and the return on investment is much, much smaller.

I live in Zone 9, which is one of the toniest districts for garden wealth. As I reported in my previous book, here's what I can collect from my backyard throughout a typical year. Note that unless it's in the "Finished" category, whatever was being harvested in the previous month continues to be available:

- **All Year**: Ready: carrots, onions (greens or bulbs), garlic (greens or bulbs), chard, lemons, sprouts

- **December, January and February:** Ready: broccoli, beets, cabbage, lettuce, oranges, parsnips, turnips

- **March and April:** Ready: snap peas, basil (indoors)

- **May:** Finished: broccoli, beets, lettuce and oranges. Ready: artichokes, celery, peaches

- **June:** Finished: artichokes, cabbage, parsnips, peaches and turnips. Ready: potatoes, tomatoes, blackberries, cucumbers, green beans, basil (outdoors)

- **July:** <u>Finished</u>: blackberries. <u>Ready</u>: corn, peppers

- **August:** <u>Ready</u>: melons

- **September and October:** <u>Finished</u>: corn and green beans. <u>Ready</u>: pumpkins, grapes, apples, ground cherries

- **November:** <u>Finished</u>: tomatoes, apples, grapes, peppers, tomatoes, potatoes, ground cherries, cucumbers, basil.

I don't like to brag, but we wealthy people do like to stick together. Send me your comments and success stories to elise@simpletonsolutions.com. I'll happily post as many as I can to the rest of our SimpletonSolutions.com community.

Keep it Simple!

Appendix A

Handy Guide to Specific Crops

Cool Crops	pH	Feeds	Plant	Notes
Artichoke	5.5-6.5	N:P:K: high	1/4", 70-80F, 10-14days	Perennial, up to 5 yrs. in temps above 14F. For food first year, grow at 32-50F for at least 250hrs. Plant 2ft apart. Before Winter, cut everything low and cover w/ mulch. Water heavily.
Asparagus	6.5-7.5	N: high P:K:mod	Buy roots	Perennial, up to 20 yrs. Bury roots 6" down and 18" apart in early Spring, or late Fall in warmer climates. First harvest in second year.
Beet	6.0-7.5	N:low P:K mod	1/2", 75-85F, 5days	Start indoors 5 wks before last frost. Outside 3" apart. Can use both beet and greens. Don't follow turnips, cabbages, bok choy, brussels sprouts.
Bok Choy	6.0-7.0	N:P:K:mod	1/4", 70-80F, 7-14 days	Start indoors 6-8wks before last frost, Transplant 6" apart. Withstands frost. Harvest outer leaves for continuous growth. Don't follow cabbages, brussels sprouts, broccoli, turnips.

Crop	pH	N:P:K	Depth, Temp, Germination	Notes
Broccoli	6.5-7.0	N:P:K:high	1/4", 75-80F, 5days	Start indoors 6-8wks before last frost. When transplanting, bury above the "bend" in the seedling. Can harvest smaller buds after main head.
Brussels sprout	6.0-7.0	N:mod P:K:high	1/4", 75-80F, 5-7days	Start indoors 6-8wks before last frost, 1' apart. Matures after 100 days, but harvest for a long time. Don't follow root crops, cabbages, broccoli, etc.
Cabbage	6.5-7.0	N:P:K:high	1/4", 75-85F, 5 days	Start indoors 4-6wks before last frost, 8" apart. Can harvest main head, then lesser heads from stalk. Don't follow root crops, broccoli, etc.
Carrot	5.5-7.0	N:mod P:K:low	1/3", 75F, 7-14days	Soak seeds overnight, then direct seed outdoors, 1/2" apart. Cover w/ clear plastic to warm and keep wet. Difficult to germinate if not wet enough.
Cauliflower	6.5-7.0	N:P:K: high	1/3", 80F, 7days	Start indoors 4-6wks before last frost, 8" apart. For white heads, keep from sun exposure 4 days before harvest. Don't follow cabbages, brussels sprouts.
Chives	6.0-7.0	N:P:K:mod	1/4", 70-80F, 7-14 days	Perennial in Zones 3-9. Can be grown indoors in pots, or transplanted outside. Slow to mature.

	pH	N:P:K	Planting	Notes
Cilantro	6.0-7.0	N:P:K:low	1/3", 55-65F, 7-10 days	Transplant 6" apart after frost. Can overwinter in warm areas. Use plants for cilantro, or allow to go to seed for coriander.
Dill	5.5-6.5	N:P:K: high	1/4", 60-70F, 7-21days	Start outdoors when soil can be worked. Attracts beneficials, so interplant with other crops.
Garlic	6.0-7.0	N:P:K:mod	2", 55F, 7 days	Plant cloves in Fall. Mulch well. Can use tender stems in recipes. When tips brown and fall over, ready for harvest. Cure bulbs outside until dry, then store.
Ground cherry	6.5-7.0	N:P:K:high	1/4", 80-85F, 10-14days	Start indoors 4 wks before last frost date. Transplant 8" apart after frost. Can be caged like tomatoes. Harvest when papery covers dry out, and fruit is shiny and yellow. Best eaten raw, but can be made into pies like cherries. Don't follow tomatos, tomatillos, peppers, eggplant.
Horseradish	6.0-7.0	N:P:K:low	Buy roots	Perennial just about everywhere. When soil 50F, bury roots 4" down. Harvest root after first hard frost.

Crop	pH	N:P:K	Depth/Temp/Days	Notes
Jerusalem 'chk	6.0-6.5	N:P:K:mod		Perennial. Plant outdoors after frost, 4" deep. Harvest tubers after hard frosts.
Kale	6.0-7.5	N:P:K:mod	1/2", 45-95F, 7days	Start indoors 6-8wks before last frost, Transplant 6" apart. Withstands frost.
Kiwi	6.0-7.0	N:P:K:mod	Buy plants or bare rooted plants in winter.	Perennial in Zones 5 and above, depending on variety. Need at least one male w/ any number of females for pollination. Like grapes, need trellising and fruit comes from one-year-old wood. Prune like grapes, too. Harvest when fruit soft in late summer, early fall.
Kohlrabi	6.0-7.5	N:P:K:mod	1/3", 50-70F, 7 days	Start outdoors when soil can be worked, 6" apart. Harvest bulbs after frost.
Lettuce	6.0-7.0	N:P:K:low	1/4", 45-50F, 5-7 days	This covers most greens and spinach. Start outdoors as soon as soil workable. Can also grow for garden window harvest indoors, but transplanting not recommended. Grow a mix of seeds for interesting salads. Harvest outer leaves for continuous harvest.

Plant	pH	Nutrients	Planting	Notes
Marjoram	6.5:7.5	N:P:K:low	1/4", 60F, 10-14 days	Start indoors 4 wks before last frost date. Transplant after frost 6" apart. Can be grown in pots. Harvest anytime once big enough to withstand plucking. Pinch out flowers.
Mint	6.0-7.0	N:P:K:mod	1/4", 60F, 10-14 days	Perennial in Zones 6 and up. Start indoors 4 wks before last frost date. Transplant after frost 6" apart. Can be grown in pots. Harvest anytime once big enough to withstand plucking. Pinch out flowers. Will spread if left unchecked.
Mushroom	6.5-7.5	N/A	N/A	Can be grown indoors or out. Frankly, this looks terrifying to me, but if you're interested, many websites have info, like fungifun.org. Can grow oysters, shiitake, wine caps and portobellos at home - so claim the sites.
Onions	6.0-7.0	N:P:K:mod	1/4", 65-85F, 5 days	Includes shallots.Transplant when soil workable, 1" apart. Can harvest stems, small onions (for thinning) or bulbs. Can grow year round in Zones 8&9. Repels pests, so interplant w/ other crops. Don't follow legumes. To store, cure outside until dry.

	pH	N:P:K	Planting	Notes
Parsnip	5.5-6.5	N: high P:K:low	1/2", 65-75F, 14days	Start outdoors when soil can be worked, 1" apart. Keep soil moist or germination won't happen. Harvest after Fall frosts. Don't follow carrots, parsley or celery.
Peas	6.0-7.0	N:P:K:low	1", 40-75F, 14 days	Plant outdoors as soon as soil workable. Harvest before peas develop much. Grow on a trellis.
Potatoes	5.5-6.5	N:P:K: high	Plant from tubers	Zones 8 and up, can plant in Fall to overwinter. Plant tuber pieces w/ eyes 4" deep when ground workable. Bury or thickly mulch all but top leaves a couple of times when growing to encourage more tuber growth. Can harvest small potatoes after flowers bloom; harvest after plant dies back. Don't follow peppers, tomatoes.
Radish	6.0-7.0	N:P:K:low	1/2", 45-80F, 10 days	Start outdoors when soil can be worked, 1" apart. Harvest at 1" diameter or more.
Rosemary	6.0-7.0	N:P:K:low	Buy plants	Perennial in Zones 8 and up. Can also be grown in a pot indoors. Plant in the spring after frost. Harvest anytime.
Rhubarb	5.5-6.5	N:P:K:low	Plant from root cutting	Perennial. Start outdoors when soil can be worked, 2' apart. Leaves are poisonous; just use the stem.

Crop	pH	N:P:K	Planting	Notes
Rutabaga	6.0-7.0	N:low P:K mod	1/2", 75F, 65-5days	Start outdoors after frost. Harvest after frost in Fall.
Salsify	6.0-7.0	N:P:K:mod	Buy roots	Roots available fall and winter. Also called "oyster plant." Two different varieties, black and white. Plant outdoors a couple of weeks before last frost, 4" apart. Harvest roots in about 120 days. Related to dandelion, so rotate with anything else.
Soybean	5.5-6.5	N:mod P:K:high	1", 75F, 10days	Start indoors 4 wks before last frost date. Transplant after frost 6" apart, on a trellis. These prefer moderate temps up to high-80's F. Harvest when fully plump.
Squash	6.0-7.0/5.5-6?	N: high P:K:mod	1", 90F, 70-7 days	Includes both summer and winter varieties: zucchini, spaghetti, pumpkins, butternut, acorn, etc. Start indoors 4 weeks before last frost date. Transplant 1' apart after soil 70F. Harvest summer squash young, winter squash when stem browns. Winter squash stores well in cool temps. Don't follow melons, cukes.

Strawberries	5.5-6.5	N:P:K:high	Buy plants	Perennial for about thee years. Different varieties can handle different climates. Transplant after soil workable. Harvest when berries are red.
Sunflowers	6.0-6.5	N:P:K:low	1", 75F, 7days	Can start indoors, but tricky to transplant. Start outdoors after frost, 6" apart. Harvest after seeds develop. Low water. Don't follow artichoke.
Tarragon	5.5-7.0	N:P:K:low	Buy plants	Perennial in Zones 4 and up. Transplant outdoors after soil 50F, 12" apart. Low watering; very drought tolerant.
Tea	6.0-6.5	N:P:K:mod	Buy plants	Ask for Camellia Sinensis online for seed or plant sources. Perennial to Zone 8. Starting from seed is difficult, and harvest will not be for 3 years.
Thyme	6.0-7.0	N:P:K:mod	Buy plants	Perennial in many zones, depending on variety. Plant 6" apart. Clip short to encourage bushiness. Pinch out flowers. Harvest anytime.

Turnip	6.0-7.0	N:P:K:low	1/3", 95F, 50-5 days	Start outdoors when soil workable, 3" apart. Can use greens and bulb. Tastes better in cool weather. Don't follow cabbages, cauliflower, brussell sprouts.
Watercress	6.0-7.5	N:P:K: high	1/4", 70?, 7days?	Start indoors 4 wks before last frost date. Transplant after frost 4" apart. Grows partially submerged, partially-shaded, preferably along streambeds. Harvest anytime, though warm weather makes it bitter.

Warm Crops	pH	Feeds	Plant	Notes
Basil	6.5-7.0	N:P:K:high	1/4", 75F, 7 days	Start indoors 4 wks before last frost date, transplant 6" apart after frost. Harvest in Summer. Keep short to encourage bushiness and keep the harvest going.
Bean	7.0-8.0	N:mod P:K:high	1", 75F, 5 days	Start indoors 4 wks before last frost date, transplant 6" apart after frost. If these are pole beans, grow up on support. Harvest in Summer when of pencil-thickness. Don't follow other legumes.
Berries, Vine	6.0-6.5	N:P:K:mod	Buy canes	Perennial. Before Winter, cut productive canes to ground level, others to 30"
Celeriac	5.5-6.5	N:P:K:high	1/4", 70F, 7days	Less finicky than celery, but takes 120-200 days. Harvest roots, not stems.
Celery	6.0-7.0	N:P:K:high	1/4", 70F, 7days	Start indoors 8-10 wks before last frost. Transplant when night temps above 40F.
Chard	6.0-7.0	N:low P:K mod	1/2", 50-85F, 7 days	Start indoors 2 wks before last frost, transplant 8" apart after frost. To harvest, can take outer leaves or cut the whole thing 1" high for continuous harvest. Can survive light frosts. Can use greens and stems. Don't follow beets or greens.

Plant	pH	N:P:K	Seed	Notes
Corn	6.0-7.0	N:P:K:high	1", 80F, 4 days	Plant outdoors, 6" apart. Water heavily once silk appears. Shade soil to keep to 65-70F. Needs lots of nitrogen. Plant w/ beans.
Cucumber	6.0-7.0	N:mod P:K:high	3/4", 80-95F, 4 days	Start indoors 3 wks before frost. Transplant 4" apart when 60F or higher at night. Trellis vines to grow upward. Pick often. Water evenly.
Eggplant	5.5-7.0	N:mod P:K:high	1/4", 85F, 7 days	Start indoors 6-8wks before last frost. Transplant when soil over 70F, 6" apart. Trellis to grow upward. Support fruits.
Fennel	6.0-7.0	N:mod P:K:low	1/4", 65-75F, 7-14 days	Transplant outside when soil 65F at least, 8" apart. Grow separately from other plants. Can use leaves, stalks and bulb.
Ginger	6.0-7.0	N:P:K: high	Buy roots	Soak in warm water overnight. Can also start suspended 1/3 in water w/ toothpicks until 1" growth. Plant in large pot, just below surface w/ buds up. Transplant in light shade outside when temps over 50F. Can use stems or roots. When weather cools, dig up and repot; keep dry for winter dormancy.

	pH	N:P:K	Planting	Notes
Grapes	6.0-6.8	N:P:K: high	Buy potted plants or bare root starts in winter	Perennial in Zones 5 and up, depending on variety. Prune in winter to remove old growth and self-choking stems. Need lots of sun. Cut back long runners. Harvest after grapes color and get soft. Can use leaves, too.
Leek	6.0-7.0	N:P:K:mod	1/4", 75F, 7 days	Start indoors 4 wks before last frost date, transplant 6" apart after frost. Harvest in Summer.
Melons	6.5-7.0	N:low,P:K:high	1/2", 80-90F, 5 days	Inc. watermelon, cantaloupe, muskmelon, honeydew... Start indoors 3 weeks before last frost date. Transplant when soil 70F. No watering when fruit ripening. Don't follow cukes or squash.
Okra	6.0-8.0	N:P:K:mod	3/4", 80-95F, 10 days	Start indoors 4 wks before last frost date, transplant 8" apart after frost. Harvest when 2" long. Eat right away.
Oregano	6.0-7.0	N:P:K:low	1/4", 60F, 7-14days	Start indoors 6-8wks before last frost. Transplant after soil 55F or more, 6" apart. Can be grown in a pot.

Parsley	6.0-7.0	N:P:K:mod	1/4", 65-80F, 3 weeks	Soak seeds overnight. Transplant when soil 60F during day. Take outer leaves for continuous harvest. Can be grown in a pot.
Peanuts	6.0-7.0	N:low P:K mod	4", 70F, 14 days	Start outdoors after last frost. Harvest a couple of months after flowers, and peanuts dry. Cure for a couple of days outside.
Peppers	5.5-7.0	N:P:K:high	1/4", 80-85F, 7days	Start indoors 6-8wks before last frost. Transplant once soil 60F at least. Can harvest from green to red in color. Don't follow potatoes or tomatoes.
Sage	5.5-6.5	N:P:Klow	1/4", 65-70F, 7-21days	Perennial for 5 years in Zones 4-8. Start indoors 6-8 weeks before last frost. Light watering. Pinch flowers. Harvest leaves.
Squash	6.0-7.0/5.5-6?	N: high P:K:mod	1", 70-90F, 7 days	Includes both summer and winter varieties: zucchini, spaghetti, pumpkins, butternut, acorn, etc. Start indoors 4 weeks before last frost date. Transplant after soil 70F. Harvest summer squash young, winter squash when stem browns. Winter squash stores well in cool temps. Don't follow melons, cukes.

	pH	N:P:K	Grow from	Description
Sweet Potatoes	5.5-6.5	N:P:K:low	Grow from tubers or slips	Put the bottom of a half of a sweet potato in water to get it to sprout. Plant the sprouts with pieces of potato separately. Start outdoors after last frost date. Harvestable after 100 or more days. Don't follow root crops.
Tomatillos	6.0-7.0	N:P:K:low	1/4". 70-80F, 10-14days	Start indoors 4 wks before last frost date, transplant 8" apart after frost. Harvest when husks split or fill out a couple of months after transplant. Don't follow tomatoes, peppers, eggplant or legumes.
Tomatoes	5.5-6.5	N:P:K:high	1/4", 80F, 7days	Start indoors 6-8wks before last frost. Transplant after soil 55F or more, 1' apart. When transplanting or repotting, bury up to all but 6" of leaves to encourage more root growth. Put in tomato cages. Don't follow eggplants, potatoes, peppers.
Yam	6.0-8.0	N:low P:K high	Buy a yam	Not to be mistaken w/ sweet potatoes, these need almost a year of frost-free growth to mature. Tropical plant. I say don't bother.

Appendix B
Highly Recommended Reading

Ball Blue Book, The Guide to Home Canning and Freezing, ©
   1994 by Alltrista Corporation, Muncie, Indiana

The Encyclopedia of Country Living, by Carla Emery, © 2003 by
   Carla Emery

The New Organic Grower, by Eliot Coleman, © 1995 by Eliot
   Coleman, Chelsea Green Publishing, White River Junction, VT

Rodale's Garden Problem Solver, by Jeff Ball, © 1988 by Jeff
   Ball, Rodale Press, Emmaus, PA

Strategic Eating, The Econovore's Essential Guide, by Elise
   Cooke, © 2008 by Elise Cooke, Outskirts Press, Denver, CO

Appendix H
Highly Recommended Resources

Index

Notes:

Notes:

Notes:

Notes:

Notes:

LaVergne, TN USA
03 January 2011
210742LV00002B/15/P